AGAINST THE GRAIN

N____ ____ IN THE HOME

WILLIAM RICHARDS

Edited by Jesse J. Marth
Designed by Pascale Vonier

Photo Credits: *Front Cover*: CLT House, designed by FMD. *Opposite Page & Back Cover*: R11 Loft, designed by Pool Leber Architekten, photography by Brigida González.

Type set in P22 Mackinac Pro

ISBN: 978-0-7643-6832-5
Printed in China

Published by Schiffer Publishing, Ltd.
4880 Lower Valley Road
Atglen, PA 19310
Phone: (610) 593-1777; Fax: (610) 593-2002
Email: info@schifferbooks.com
Web: www.schifferbooks.com

For our complete selection of fine books on this and related subjects, please visit our website at www.schifferbooks.com. You may also write for a free catalog.

Schiffer Publishing's titles are available at special discounts for bulk purchases for sales promotions or premiums. Special editions, including personalized covers, corporate imprints, and excerpts, can be created in large quantities for special needs. For more information, contact the publisher.

CONTENTS

FOREWORD

In my career I have been exposed to hundreds of industry professionals in the architecture, design, and construction space. The first time I had the pleasure to work with William Richards, one of those notable professionals, it was for a presentation at the American Institute of Architects annual conference. I was floored by the thoughtful approach he took to his panel in order to create a narrative that was able to provide the audience with an entertaining version of a very complex topic.

In these pages, as a reader, you will find the same thoughtfulness as William wanders around the globe to share examples of the beauty, efficiency, and sustainability of mass timber, weaving together these messages through a variety of different projects, styles, and locations.

The following pages are filled with information portraying the intricacies of mass timber through smart designs defying conventional approaches that come together to bring better understanding of this material and its values and benefits to the industry at large.

It's truly a pleasure to read this celebration of the applications of mass timber and how it can be applied to our homes. Through insights from visionaries at the forefront of this transformative movement, each case is an extraordinary statement, boldly testing the boundaries of home design and expanding the horizons of mass timber's performance capabilities.

I have been honored to keep in touch with William through my studies of this space, relying on him specifically for his knowledge and expertise on this topic at a time when the world is at a pivotal moment where the urgency for sustainable practices is imperative.

I am sure that from this piece of work, the industry will fall in love with mass timber as a testament to human ingenuity blended with technological advancements. From there, others will take steps into new uses, adopting it into new designs and exploring it as a realistic solution to bring efficiency, beauty, and sustainability to home design.

—Jennifer Castenson

INTRODUCTION

Tipping the scales on mass timber

Before a sense of purpose within architecture, there's always a burgeoning sense of possibility—about materials, processes, applications, and invention. The story of mass timber is no different, and while much of that story has been influenced by the race to build ever taller with timber, there's another story about innovation at a smaller, residential scale that has driven the industry—and architectural innovation—to greater heights too.

Mass timber describes a category of composite materials that are derived from timber and strengthened to give them greater structural capabilities to build taller than timber frame construction normally allows. Mass timber is also a strategy to limit the carbon footprint of building activities in several ways—by sequestering carbon in timber's fibers, by fabricating panels and beams off-site and thereby reducing the number of on-site construction days, and by being a durable companion for those who live within its walls. There are also biophilic benefits to living with wood rather than the industrial materials such as glass, steel, concrete, and the most-common interior finishes: drywall, gypsum board, plasterboard, and wallboard (depending on the region of the world you live in). "Massive timber" is dominated by cross-laminated timber panels (CLT) and glued-laminated timber beams (glulam), made possible when small pieces of lumber are bonded with glue, making them strong enough to replace steel and concrete while producing a fraction of the carbon, and dramatically reducing the carbon footprint of a building compared to those that are made with conventional materials. Panels and beams created with these pieces of laminated lumber are fabricated at mills, transported to jobsites, and hoisted into place with a crane—a process that also dramatically reduces the construction time of the structure from months to weeks, or from weeks to mere days.

Since some of the CLT panels and glulam beams may be reused later in the "circular economy" of materials, a mass timber building's carbon footprint may be largely negated. Mass timber buildings are easier to insulate and climatize than buildings made with cinder blocks, pressure-treated two-by-fours, drywall, and off-the-shelf fiberglass insulation. Mass timber buildings also offer a more predictable and controllable slow burn during a fire than conventional materials, making them more fire resistant for longer.

The last decade has been a long road for its advocates, manufacturers, and architects passionate about its potential— overcoming the two-hour fire rating, creating a network of resources to share information, and convincing clients that renewables are well worth the initial investment, which is higher than more-conventional modes of construction.

Critics say that building tall with timber must be questioned in the long run, even if there is much to be gained in the short term by creating new opportunities for mass timber products to flex their capabilities. That's because sustainable forestry has to be a concerted and unified effort to ethically manage supply while architects and builders drum up demand. What is mass timber, then? In the largest sense, mass timber represents a strategy to decarbonize the building industry, which is often measured by how tall we can go with it—and how many tall buildings we can make with it. Increasingly, though, mass timber insiders are looking to measure it in other ways to address broader economic and environmental goals.

The architect Joseph Mayo's *Solid Wood: Case Studies in Mass Timber Architecture, Technology, and Design* (2015) was an ambitious look at the state of a percolating industry. For an outsider, reading Mayo's book sets the bar for other books by asking, "So, what are we talking about here?" and "What does it mean to contemplate a timber building when most of our output as a society is steel and concrete?" As a coda to Mayo's book, Lindsay Wikstrom's *Designing the Forest* (2023) answered the "So what" question in myriad ways. So what if we can achieve twenty stories with mass timber; what about sustainable forestry? So what if code officials say we can; can the supply chain manage it? It's a sobering set of questions that several design firms have attempted to answer too, some of which have played out in a spate of monographs that had appeared in the last half decade.

One of them, *Timber in Architecture* (2022), chronicled Shigeru Ban's experiments and triumphs with wood structures that were tectonically daring, combining real craftsmanship with industrial efficiencies—and elevating his airports, gymnasia, houses, and museums to the realm of poetry. Another one, *Mass Timber: Design and Research* (2018), written by the architect Susan Jones, offers a set of deeply personal perspectives—not just the achievements—that demonstrate how mass timber as a material focus drives Jones's fertile and thriving design practice. Ask anyone in mass timber and they'll tell you that she has, almost single-handedly, galvanized an entire industry over the course of fifteen years through her relentless advocacy of timber, not to mention her code authorship, teaching, and lecturing. Her book offers a singular guide—and a gift—for those who follow in her footsteps.

Waugh Thisleton's twenty-nine-unit Murray Grove (2009) in the Hackney neighborhood of London is the first tall urban housing project to be constructed from prefabricated solid timber. It went up in just forty-nine weeks.

Yet, so much of mass timber's media coverage over the last fifteen years has been about the sprint to the top of the pile—building tall was about creating explicit metrics for "massive timber" to beat steel. It has been the cause célèbre of design media, whose writers heralded new heights at every step of the way—Waugh Thisleton's Murray Grove (nine stories, 2009) and Dalston Works (ten stories, 2017), both in London; Shigeru Ban's Tamedia Office Building in Zurich (seven stories, 2013); Michael Green Architecture's T3 in Minneapolis (seven stories, 2016), Voll Arkitekter's Mjøstårnet in Brumunddal, Norway (eighteen stories, 2019) and famously profiled in the *New Yorker*; and Jean-Paul Viguier & Associates' Hypérion tower in Bordeaux (eighteen stories, 2022). Also at press time, Zaha Hadid Architects had recently won approval to design and build Eco Park, a five-thousand-seat timber stadium along the M5 motorway near Gloucester, England, and Venhoeven CS and Atelier 2/3/4's Centre Aquatique Olympique was completed in 2024 outside Saint-Denis north of Paris, a six-thousand-seat venue for the games that adapts for smaller crowds and activities including rock-climbing and fitness classes to permanently serve the region's residents.

Three existential challenges for mass timber

Mass timber has come a long way, and the achievements of its architects and builders to date reflect two simultaneous existential challenges for mass timber. The first challenge centered on the question "Could we ameliorate embodied carbon by engineering and deploying a safe, effective material that matched the strength of steel?" The second challenge reflected the delta among the industry's ambition, building- and fire-code adoption, and client readiness (not to mention lender willingness). Perhaps the strongest piece of evidence that these challenges have been met is the International Code Council's (ICC) 2021 update to its International Building Code (IBC) to include mass timber up to eighteen stories or 270 feet tall. If "ever taller" was the proving ground, then mass timber's enshrinement in a model building code that municipalities may adopt was the proof—included as part of the "heavy timber" type, one of five types recognized by the IBC, which calls for wood structures that can withstand fires for longer than standard wooden structures. The columns and beams of Type IV heavy timber structures, per the model code, must be at least 8 inches thick. Floor planks must be 6 inches thick. Exterior walls must be made of noncombustible materials, relegating mass timber to the structure and interior finishes only at larger scales.

Even if the IBC update reflects the allowances already made in municipalities around the world, a lot of other cities are trying to catch up to the idea that CLT at larger scales is a good idea. Some, like Bordeaux, France, are all in, while others have gingerly approached the issue, such as New York City, with its 85-foot rule for mass timber construction. The use of CLT or glulam at ever-larger scales in concert with a concrete podium, in tandem with glazing, and often in league with steel is a story of transformation—and the family of products that constitute mass timber is far less of a novelty now than it ever has been in the last generation and is becoming a practical and desirable solution.

In the contemporary architectural sense, mass timber has been an exciting field of experimentation for more than twenty years. Importantly, it's become a more inclusive field in the last decade, as more and more architects have been able to take advantage of robust supply chains and myriad manufacturers—creating an environmental benefit that's tangible and measurable. The Softwood Lumber Board and other industry groups measure progress in terms of demand, in board-feet, for mass timber products and also how many metric tons of carbon dioxide were sequestered by those products. In 2022, 5.3 million metric tons of CO_2 were captured, stored, and thereby kept out of the environment thanks to CLT, glulam, and the like—the rough equivalent of keeping every single car registered in the District of Columbia parked for five years. (That figure is up from 4.9 million in 2021 and 4.5 million in 2020.) Still, others measure progress by how many "tall" timber buildings are completed in a given period of time, defined by anything over eight stories. Between 2017 and the pandemic in 2020, thirty-two all-timber or hybrid-timber buildings were completed worldwide of eight stories or more, which is about as many as were completed in the entire decade before,

"Paimio" lounge chair, model no. 41, 1931–1932. Alvar Aalto, designer. Laminated birch, bent plywood.

according to the Council on Tall Buildings and Urban Habitat. Things took a turn during the pandemic (as it did for much of the design and construction industry) but recently there have been promising results that will bring mass timber back in line with its once-aggressive trajectory.

But the idea that one can strengthen wood to achieve daring structural—or sculptural—ends is not a new one. In the contemporary architectural sense, it goes back to the Finnish architect Alvar Aalto's experiments in the 1920s and 1930s with plywood, such as, famously, a lounge chair for the Paimio Tuberculosis Sanitorium. Architects still look to Aalto, as well as others who were just as venturesome, prefiguring today's laminated-timber projects at larger scales such as Alfred Beach's prototype railway tube for the London Underground in 1867; or the bestselling, Michigan-made Haskell canoe in 1917; or the U.S. Forest Products Laboratory's plywood house that debuted in 1936. What Alvar Aalto accomplished with plywood still challenges designers today working at the leading edge of material science, and, thanks to Rhino or Revit, it's also an approachable challenge.

The productization of those other examples also raises questions about economic viability for today's engineered-wood heirs. It's one thing to manufacture a hundred canoes a month to meet demand in the heady years before the Great Depression. It's another to design and build a hundred homes in today's economic climate. In fact, there isn't a single architect alive who has designed and built a hundred single-family mass timber homes (or even half that many).

Several architects whose projects are profiled in this book would know. They all bought their respective plots of land,

Milwaukee's crown jewel, the 284-foot-tall Ascent, designed by Korb + Associates with structural engineers Thornton Thomasetti, was the world's tallest mass timber building at press time. Here, as with most mass timber projects big and small, the CLT and glulam are left exposed.

they all designed their respective houses, and they all financed the construction of those houses. While they represent the ideal architect to advise clients on how things really work with prefabricated engineered wood products, the variables for mass timber—from sourcing to shipping to transportation to renting the crane, to coordinating the delivery, to finding a skilled contractor who can physically assemble the panels—are formidable.

Building with mass timber is still an act of courage on the part of everyone involved, and if its industry's development has proven anything, it's that courage can be more than its own reward. It can lead to a real return on investment when it comes to carbon neutrality because of the way wood captures CO_2 in its fibers. It's not to say that mass timber is a panacea that will single-handedly decarbonize the built environment. But it is to say that mass timber can contribute mightily to decarbonization by reducing the embodied carbon of what gets designed and built.

Mass timber at residential scales

At the single-family residential scale, mass timber has long been considered a novelty because it's an expensive strategy requiring a large investment relative to the overall cost of the project. One study published by the US Department of Agriculture in 2020 measured mass timber to have a 26 percent higher front-end cost than a similar building completed in concrete. The study's authors looked at what it would take to complete a hypothetical twelve-story building in Portland, Oregon, which is "tall" in industry parlance and also in an area of the country that has an established supply pipeline, not to mention a critical mass of designers and contractors who are versed in the use of CLT, glulam, and its ilk.

But what about at the scale of a two-story single-family residential project? Jennifer Bonner (who designed, built, and owned Haus Gables, which appears in this book) once told me she reckons the front-end cost of mass timber can certainly be 20–30 percent higher than something in concrete (and steel), or even as high as 40–50 percent depending on the circumstances.

"You're going to get pushback because it's more expensive than a traditional house," says Bonner, "but guess what? We're not building solid houses in America any more. These are solid houses. This is a good direction for American homes to go in. But because of the upcharge on mass timber, that's why multifamily makes sense. That's why tall buildings make sense. But we have to make single-family homes and small multifamily homes work with CLT."

Comparing mass timber's application for single-family homes to multifamily developments, one thing I've heard from architects is that mass timber products have an economic golden ratio. The more residential units you clump together, the easier it is to absorb the cost of mass timber's manufacture, delivery, and assembly. Ty Tikari, the California-born, London-based architect-owner-developer whose Rye Apartments are also profiled in this book, says it's somewhere around eight to ten units. Others have told me five units is a good number, so long as shipping costs aren't out of control. Still others say fifteen is ideal, especially if you can offer a variety of floor plans that attract a range of buyers or renters. At those tipping points, the 20 or 30 percent higher front-end costs of using mass timber disappear when you can significantly reduce the length of time it takes to finish the building. Months are whittled down to weeks—depending on the scale and location. The costs also go down when you significantly reduce the number of on-site laborers. Instead of having thirty workers pouring concrete, you can have nine carpenters assembling CLT panels.

Andrew Waugh, cofounder and principal of London's Waugh Thistleton Architects, a pioneering firm in mass timber, says the question is not about cost in the end, because it's a vague number masquerading as a firm one. He says affordability is a better barometer to adjudge mass timber's viability.

"There's no reason why it shouldn't be affordable," says Waugh. "We do an ongoing analysis of our buildings, which [number] thirty now, and the mass timber itself never takes up more than 21 to 24 percent of the budget, from supply to erection. If someone tells you their budget problem is mass timber, they're just blaming mass timber for some other problem."

US Forest Service rangers are the lucky test subjects for PathHouse, a prototype by Ben Kaiser and LSW Architects for a modular home that can expand to meet demands or remain a small efficiency cabin.

Kaiser and LSW hope to complete thirty-seven units as part of a pilot project in the near future.

For that reason, the single-family residential sphere has long been considered an experimental zone for architects and builders, some of whom put up the money themselves and went deeply into the red as a result. It's also been an experimental zone for agencies and institutions that can more easily absorb the cost of innovation than private owners and developers, which has paved an ever-widening path to imagine mass timber as a solution for affordable housing and emergency housing that's either modular or nonmodular in its construction. The US Department of Housing and Urban Development's annual showcase on the National Mall in Washington, DC, raises awareness of affordable-housing solutions and new technologies that, at scale, can make homes more efficient and, indeed, affordable. The exhibitors represent hemp insulation kiosks, hydronic-heat-transfer demonstrations, printed homes, tiny homes, homes for disabled veterans, and trailer homes. Two mass timber homes located next to each other on the Mall in 2023 represented modular building and scalable solutions for permanent and affordable housing—both funded by the US Forest Service.

One of them, PathHouse, is a prototype for a modular home designed to be added on to on the basis of the homeowner's long-term needs, and is the product of a manufacturing partnership between Ben Kaiser and LSW Architects. As a prototype, Kaiser and LSW have styled it as an efficiency cabin, like the kind you might find beside a lake in Maine or Minnesota. You enter into a small kitchen, eating area, and living area, and through a small hallway are two bedrooms, which would be ideal for a family of three, four, or even five who might need emergency housing in the wake of a disaster. It's also ideal for the PathHouse prototype's target client for the time being: US Forest Service rangers.

Kaiser and LSW hope to complete thirty-seven such homes as part of a pilot project to house rangers in somewhat far-flung places quickly and easily, making the expandable format of the modular studio, one-, two-, or three-bedroom PathHouses particularly useful to adapt to immediate and long-term staffing needs. It's also particularly fast to put up—or at least it's intended to be, with all the systems moved out of the walls and into the floor, meaning that all MEP work could be done ahead of the panel deliveries, making on-site assembly more efficient than it already is with more-conventional mass timber projects.

Beyond Kaiser and LSW offering deployable ranger stations for its initial funder, the firm's two other goals for PathHouse are related, in part to attract other funders and in part to scale up: get other architects to work with PathHouse as a manufacturing strategy and get other agencies to work with Path-House as an affordable-housing solution. In both cases, the potential of PathHouse (the prototype) is tied to PathHouse (the company) in its ability to open regional manufacturing facilities that will start with one hundred to five hundred units per year and, ultimately, 192 units per day (or 46,000 per year). At that scale, the affordability aspect of this "affordable" solution starts to kick in, and Kaiser estimates they will be able to offer a base module—equivalent to a 250-square-foot studio—for $49,000 to $52,000. Additional bedroom modules would cost less, since they won't need plumbing or electrical for appliances, presumably bringing a one-to-two-bedroom house into the $125,000 range, which is significantly less expensive than a basic, conventionally built house at a similar square footage.

Next door at HUD's housing exposition, Timber Age Systems, based in Durango, Colorado, showcased its panelized modular-housing solution by using a prototype that they had actually sold to a client as an office, a barely 100-square-foot ponderosa pine CLT structure. (The owner graciously agreed to let it be trucked to DC from Durango before taking possession of his new writing studio.) Timber Age is also ready to scale up, and what the company learned by building the office/studio module, they have already applied to their next two projects—a library and a 2,000-square-foot home.

Importantly, all of their work is within 100 miles of their manufacturing site in southwestern Colorado—the trees, the mill, and the building sites.

"When we started, we advertised ourselves as a CLT manufacturer. We knew we'd never make panels big enough in a skyscraper, but that's okay because we're not building skyscrapers in Durango," says Kyle Hanson, Timber Age's founder and CEO. "So, when I started to think about the residential context, CLT was already being used in PassivHaus projects, so that became a building block in our bigger mission. It helped us step back and think about what we wanted to achieve, which are communities that can make high-performance and durable homes that take a bite out of carbon emissions. Every municipality should get on board with that."

Ponderosa pine doesn't make for very good dimensional lumber, which dominates the conventional homebuilding industry, but it does suit CLT panels that can smooth out its defects. The other advantage is that it's inexpensively obtained in the Durango area.

"We asked ourselves all sorts of questions about what was feasible and what wasn't," says Hanson, "and from the time our wood leaves the forest about 20 miles from us, where we're paying firewood prices or less, we get it and put it back into a structure that we're delivering 40–60 miles from us."

The company's ultimate goal is modular mass timber for mass housing, with the same regional strategy as PathHouse, but with an important distinction: Timber Age wants to utilize the locally available timber in each region, rather than standardizing the material for all regions. By identifying the local supply and setting up a local sawmill—estimating that start-up cost to be $1 million per mill—they reckon they can spin out exactly enough 10 × 5 ft. panels (each at 3 in. thick) to satisfy demand while also limiting their risk. Since regions have surpluses of wood, or perhaps surpluses of mixed woods that aren't in and of themselves useful or desirable as construction materials, Timber Age can target it, take it, and spin literal gold out of straw.

"It's important for this to start as small as possible and be in balance with what the forest can produce," says Hanson. "There will be places where what we do isn't the answer. This isn't a panacea. We will not supply the world with our product."

Enter mass timber's third existential challenge, which its industry is grappling with today: not "What do we do?" with mass timber now that we've figured out the industry, but rather "To what end?"

If we've figured out the codes and the value chain for mass timber production, then to what end is it supremely useful? Is it a viable alternative to steel at anything below twenty-five stories (or roughly 82 meters)? Certainly.

Can its rapid fabrication and construction time efficiently deliver sorely needed market rate and affordable housing?

Absolutely.

Is it still a viable alternative no matter how far the timber has to travel to get there? That depends—and a strong case can be made for a lengthy supply chain for large-scale projects with a broader benefit such as factories, data centers, warehouses, and fulfillment facilities.

But if we're talking about the question "To what end?," many in the industry—and certainly the authorities in charge of city, county, state, and federal housing incentives—see a stronger case to employ mass timber as both a time-saving construction strategy and decarbonization strategy. As a society, we've tried "shelter at all costs," and it has too often resulted in substandard structures with a shelf life, using materials that imperiled our environment. That's true of large-scale public housing and that's true of developer-driven sub-urban tract housing. Mass timber is about more than asking if the cost is worth it. It's about asking if the carbon is worth it. If shelter remains as elemental to architecture's fundamental purpose as anything else, then mass timber must become as purposeful as possible in sheltering our planet and ourselves.

HAUS GABLES

Atlanta, Georgia, USA
Jennifer Bonner / MALL
2019

Atlanta annexed its first five wards in 1854, seven years after the city's incorporation, forming a pinwheel plan centered on a no-man's-land railroad interchange once known as the Gulch. Atlanta's origin story is less dramatic than Tenochtitlán's, but no less auspicious—in place of an eagle consuming a snake perched on a cactus, Atlantans remember a spike driven into the dirt by the Macon and Western Railroad to create the old Circle Wye downtown railroad junction. The Reconstruction Era added two more wards to make seven, followed by an orderly conversion of older wards into newer, bigger ones numbered according to the familiar pinwheel pattern that was, for many years, contained within a perfect circle on the map. Later acquisitions have given us Atlanta's familiar shape today—irregular and knobby in the mode of Vienna or Paris, but with a clear center and periphery. Atlanta's twentieth-century urban development patterns were laid during Reconstruction, but its explosion in the twenty-first century to become the largest metropolis in the Southeast is a growth story we've seen before in Detroit and Cleveland—once unbound juggernauts and now memento mori. (Today, we continue to see that story unfolding in the quad-county area that defines greater Los Angeles.) Atlanta's Beltline greenway clearly highlights that periphery today, tracing a permeable boundary for wildlife and joggers alike that faintly resembles a chipped arrowhead in plan.

"My claim about building this way is about this: if we're going to build on dense parcels, our footprint will be small, which means we need to have a volumetric interior. It needs to feel grander than it is by the footprint," says the architect Jennifer Bonner.

The story of Atlanta's 2,200-square-foot Haus Gables isn't about sprawl at all, but about making the most of a modest site—contravening the city's tendency to spread out. In an eclectic neighborhood of Cape Cods, bungalows, and unclassifiable multifamily piles, the streetside facade has the basic form of a Dutch rowhouse. But the unadorned white-painted, cross-laminated timber in place of bricks and punched-out windows in irregular patterns offers the first clue that this house might be different, as does its gabled end of a roof that's not centered, but askew, revealing its southern flank. A generous yard runs along the north façade to the back of the site, which reveals the true nature of the house to the passerby: this is a sculpture and a house in relation to each other; this is resistance and conformity in relation to suburban idyll.

Bonner's exuberant, polygonal ceilings make us
feel as if we're passing through—and able to live
within—a mountain's peaks.

If architect Jennifer Bonner's chief design constraint was the lot size, then her chief design strategy was counterpoise—to create a home cathedral for a Bertoia cathedra, and to create a sense of grandeur through interior volume, befitting the Atlanta of architects John Portman, Roche and Dinkaloo, and Johnson and Burgee, whose tall downtown buildings have come to symbolize the city for fifty million visitors each year. Entering through the garage, in a nod to the architect Le Corbusier's vision of convenience, and after climbing to the second floor near the far western corner of the house, you're drawn straight through to the far eastern corner by the cathedral ceiling above the dining room midway through the space. It's the first glimpse of what's on the third floor, where, vaulting above the midline of the interior, Bonner's exuberant, polygonal ceilings make us feel as though we're passing through—and able to live within—a mountain's peaks.

For Bonner, they're more like the inside of pointy party caps—part of a prior exhibition installation called "Domestic Hats," for which she combined the dormers, A-frames, and shed roofs found throughout Atlanta's wards and created a series of variants in the form of architectural-massing models. That's the origin of Haus Gables—what she calls a "roof plan"—working downward to give the space a logic.

"My claim about building this way is about this: If we're going to build on dense parcels, our footprint will be small, which means we need to have a volumetric interior. It needs to feel grander than it is by the footprint," says Bonner, making a nod to what she calls Portman's soaring "super atrium" for the Hyatt Regency a mile away. "That's the typology—the super atrium—and I hoped to invent something here like that."

To translate the roof plan into the starting point for a livable space, Bonner needed to create vaulted ceilings for the third floor without cross beams and trusses perched over the home's primary living space, second bedroom, and catwalk overlooking the dining table below (and providing access to the third-floor balcony). She designed the home's three-ply, five-ply, and seven-ply cross-laminated timber panels, which were cut from 9-by-50-foot pieces over the course of three days by KLH Massivholz in Austria and shipped on three containers to the Port of Savannah, where they were loaded on trucks for the 243-mile journey to Atlanta.

Austrian companies remain Europe's largest supplier of mass timber products and have a significant market share in North America, but Bonner first approached a Canadian supplier for her panels, with the idea that their journey across the country on an eighteen-wheeler might be more carbon friendly than a cross-Atlantic trek. In the end, the supplier's struggle to work with her nonstandard peaks that distinguish Haus Gables conceptually and, among its neighbors in Atlanta, pushed her to seek out KLH, on the advice of her structural engineer, Hanif Kara. (On-site, Bonner's installation team was led by Terry Ducatt, who also worked on Susan Jones's home in Seattle, CLTHouse.) Despite pivoting to a new fabricator nearly 5,000 miles away, Bonner was committed to creating a new horizon for CLT in custom residential design as both architect and owner—and in occupying both roles, Haus Gables was as personal as a project could be. Noticeably, the fixtures and finishes aren't Scandinavian inspired, as is so often the case with mass timber interiors, but rather extensions to Bonner's own sense of style and her championing of what she calls "faux-finishes" that are familiar backdrops at the intersection of American pop culture and domestic traditions. Marbled, speckled, and veiny vinyl and terrazzo tiles in black, white, mustard yellow, robin's-egg blue, and magenta mingle with the warm blond hues of the CLT and the ash-gray, concrete, and pearl patinas of the home's different floors. It's about as far from Oslo as you can get, and although Bonner and her family sold it after it was completed, Haus Gables remains her stake in the ground for CLT's possibilities.

"CLT was so wonderful to work with, and it has reshaped how I think about designing and building. I put five years of my life into it—there was no client, and it's all my ideas. Nobody was going to call me and ask for a CLT house, so I had to do it myself."

Marbled, speckled, and veiny vinyl and terrazzo
tiles mingle with the ash-gray, concrete, and pearl
patinas of the home's different floors. All offer a
counterpoint to the CLT's elemental look and feel.

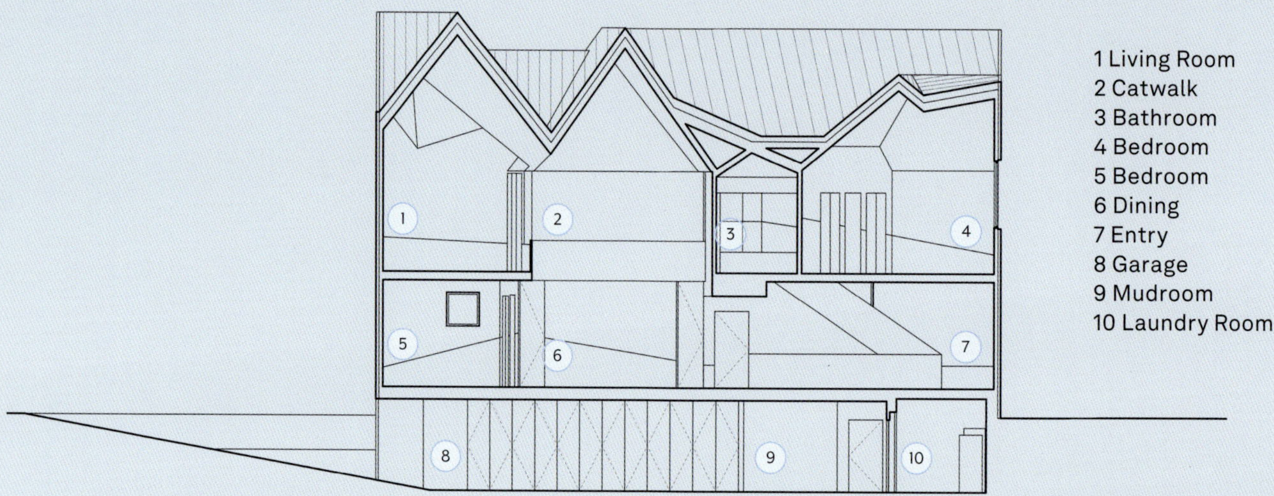

1 Living Room
2 Catwalk
3 Bathroom
4 Bedroom
5 Bedroom
6 Dining
7 Entry
8 Garage
9 Mudroom
10 Laundry Room

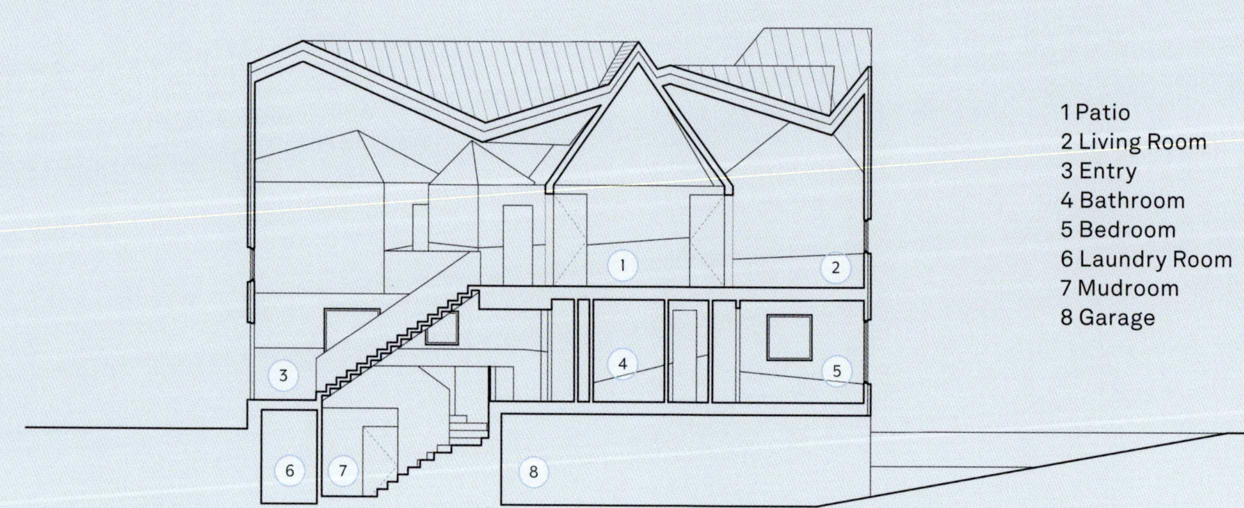

1 Patio
2 Living Room
3 Entry
4 Bathroom
5 Bedroom
6 Laundry Room
7 Mudroom
8 Garage

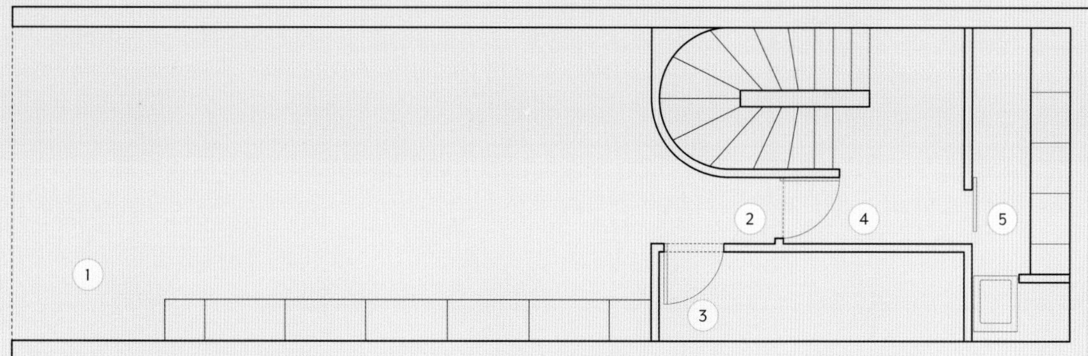

LEVEL 1 • BASEMENT
1 Garage
2 Entry
3 Mechanical Room
4 Mudroom
5 Laundry Room

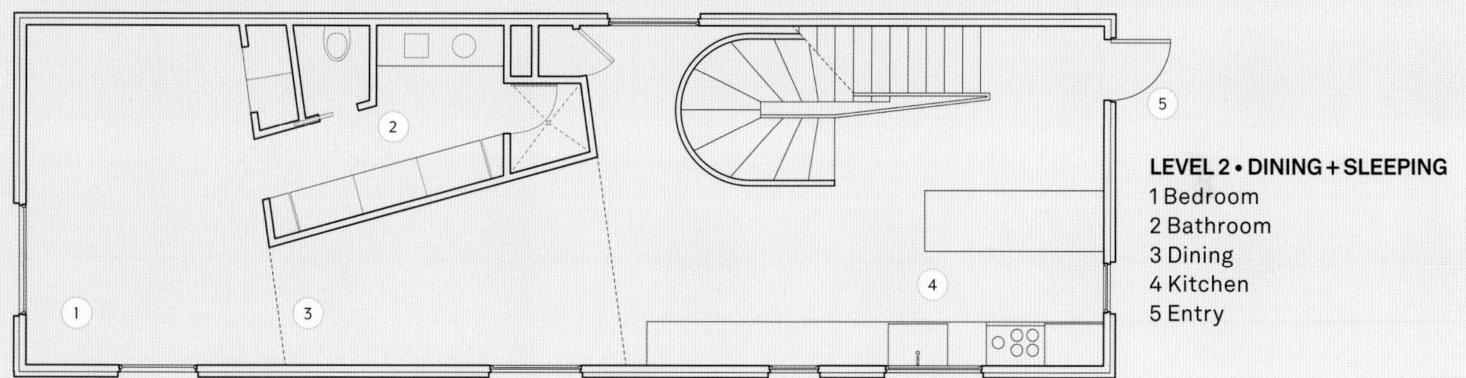

LEVEL 2 • DINING + SLEEPING
1 Bedroom
2 Bathroom
3 Dining
4 Kitchen
5 Entry

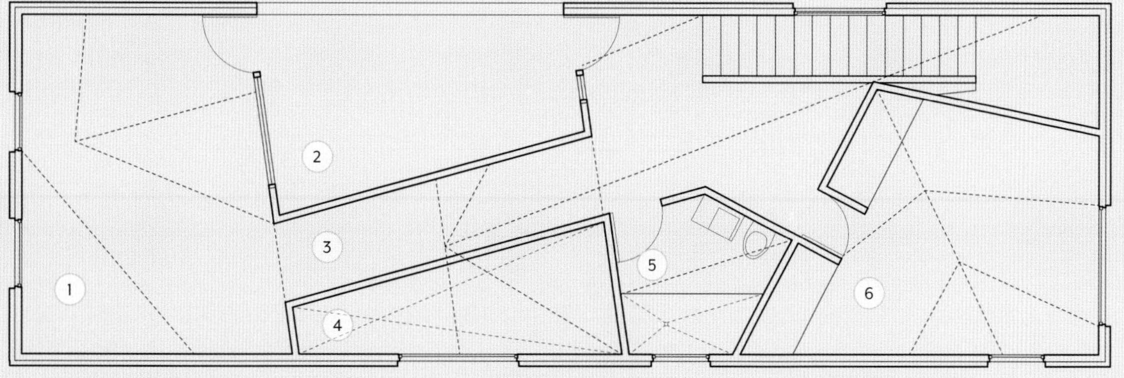

LEVEL 3 • LIVING + SLEEPING
1 Living Room
2 Patio
3 Catwalk
4 Double-Height Space
5 Bedroom

MAURER RESIDENCE

British Columbia, Canada
Florian Maurer
2003, 2020

Architect Florian Maurer designed and built his home in the Okanagan Valley, along the southern flank of British Columbia, with three motives in mind. "To be happy. To have a garden. To make a contribution to architecture," he says about the 1,950-square-foot glue-laminated timber home perched on a steel base overlooking Okanagan Lake.

Maurer used glulam as the basis of a superstructure for a modest home formed by beams and posts—a purist's delight, which he says was his nod to highbrow architectural theory. For the Munich native, whose parents were both orthodox modernists, function and economy might have started as architectural goals, but they ended up being the chief strategy to achieve something livable.

"Buildings that don't make us happy are unsustainable for me," he says, "and architecture has to make us happy."

Drilled into bedrock and cosseted by succulent plants, the Maurer Residence and its extension appears lighter than its rigorous geometry suggests.

The project unfolded in two phases over nearly twenty years: an original home, studio, and garden for the Maurers completed in 2004, and a gallery and media-space addition for new owners completed in 2020. The difference between old and new is apparent if you're looking for it, but taken together, the entire suite of buildings arranged along the brow of the hill speaks of one design parti: the procession from public to private spaces, which are clearly legible in the site plan and in the path one takes from street to cliff's edge.

On the inside looking out, generous windows in the original house and floor-to-ceiling glazing in the art gallery and media-space addition create a sense of prospect and refuge that many homes possess, but few as dramatically as Maurer's house—save for, say, Philip Johnson's Glass House in New Canaan, Connecticut, or Ludwig Mies van der Rohe's Farnsworth House in Plano, Illinois.

Over nearly twenty years, the house has been a laboratory for both the original architect, Florian Maurer, and the addition's managing architect, Austin Hawkins.

Yet, neither Johnson nor Farnsworth courts the Burkean sublime as Maurer does, who created more than a home where the walls dissolve into the commanding viewshed to the west. Behind the house and gallery's bedrock perch is an extensive wild garden of native plantings and a smaller vegetable garden, as well as a studio and carport that defines the eastern lot line, which meets the road. There's more living space outdoors to amble around than there is indoors, in fact, beneath the stands of Ponderosa pines that dot the property.

"This house is modest in size but very spacious because the circulation space is outside," says Maurer, "and by using the land only as you need to use it, and by building only what you need, it's the most important aspect of sustainability that most people don't think about. Sustainability isn't certification and ratings. It's common sense."

Maurer completed the studio, carport, garden, and original home for him and his wife, Erika, and lived there for more than a decade before selling it. But when its new owners wanted to expand the project to include the dramatically perched art gallery and media space, they returned to Maurer's firm, f2a, during a time when the Maurers were decamping to Italy. F2a principal Austin Hawkins took the reins as project architect on the addition.

"This house is modest in size but very spacious because the circulation space is outside," says Maurer, "and by using the land only as you need to use it, and by building only what you need, it's the most important aspect of sustainability that most people don't think about. Sustainability isn't certification and ratings. It's common sense."

"A key aspect in engineering spans is that it's important to do only what you need to—it has to be precise and minimal," says Austin Hawkins of the addition. "The joinery is tight and it performs well—and there's nothing extra and there's no fluff."

On the outside looking in, the addition's superstructure connects with the ground in very few places atop spindly piers drilled into the bedrock and cosseted at ground level by succulent plants, making the home's massing appear far lighter than it actually is—made possible by the post-and-beam glulam superstructure.

"A key aspect in engineering spans is that it's important to do only what you need to—it has to be precise and minimal," says Hawkins, who credits glulam manufacturer StructureLam (based in Penticton, British Columbia) for working with f2a to create an addition that's as well built as Maurer's original, handbuilt home, defined by a 7-foot-grid module (or 2.2 meters). "The joinery is tight and it performs well—and there's nothing extra and there's no fluff," says Hawkins, noting that the geothermal heating loop under the addition makes the home nearly energy free.

Maurer and Hawkins used glulam as the basis of the superstructure, formed by beams and posts throughout the original home and the new gallery addition.

The photovoltaic solar panel system also helps harvest energy, and the property is able to produce 70 percent of what's needed on-site.

Going back to Maurer's three motives—to be happy, to have a garden, and to contribute to architecture—it's a trinity in which satisfaction and productivity are intertwined, where enjoying repose and having purpose are mutually supportive. You can see it in the procession from public to private spaces on the deep site, relating to a premodern European model of the workshop frontage or forecourt and a home in the back, or relating to the Roman domus, with its outer walls and inner atrium. For Maurer, that agreement between public and private, and the zones we create in our homes to enforce it, also relates to the courtyard homes of Argentina or Mexico—often with two levels, and an inner balcony.

It's what Maurer calls an introverted concept. "I wanted to build around a wonderful place inside that is protected and creates controlled views of the outside," he says. "It's about creating a barrier, but also being open at the same time."

Still, the vegetable and wildflower plots that mediate between front-of-site studio and back-of-site house, especially in the context of satisfaction and productivity as mutually supportive dimensions of domestic life, offer yet another way of interpreting what the Maurer Residence is about. In his 1964 book, *The Machine in the Garden*, the historian Leo Marx created an enduring framework to consider the pastoral ideal in literature in light of the exigencies of modern life, notably industry. The two—machine and garden—might be opposed to one another, but that should not require us to choose between them as an either/or proposition, according to Marx. Rather, the tension between them is actually worthwhile— and can be an engine of placemaking.

Embedded in placemaking, Maurer's motives to create a home for himself seem perfectly at home in the final outcome.

1 Addition
2 Lake View across Roof
3 Lake View
4 Existing Ponderosa Pines
5 Main House
6 Bedrook Outcrop
7 Veggie Garden
8 Wild Garden
9 Primary Bedroom
10 Garage
11 Studio

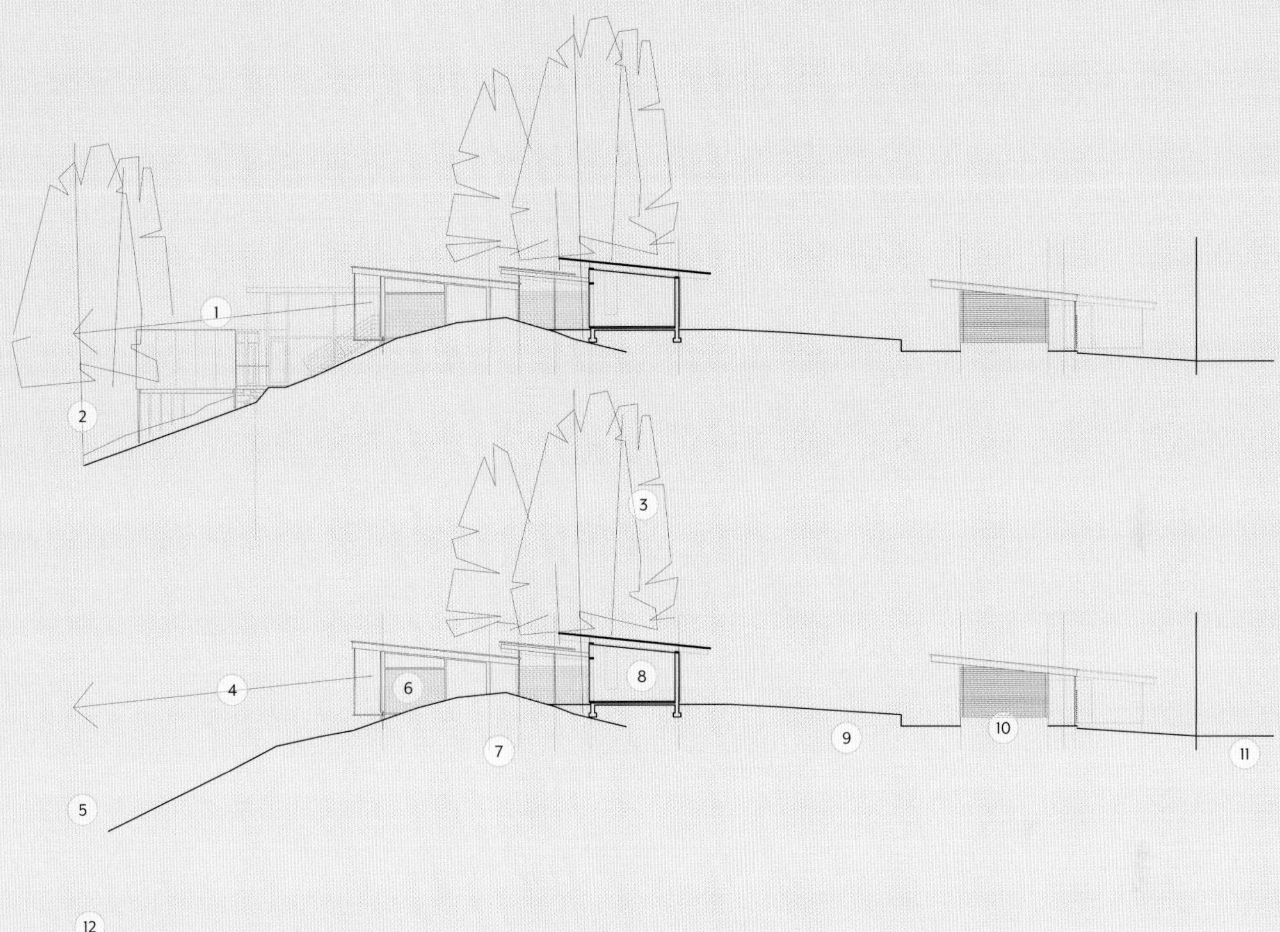

1 Lake View across Roof
2 South View with Addition
3 Existing Ponderosa Pines
4 Lake View
5 Original South View
6 Main House
7 Bedrook Outcrop
8 Primary Bedroom
9 Garden
10 Studio
11 Access Road
12 South Views before and after Addition

BRIDGE HOUSE

British Columbia, Canada
Etienne de Villiers
2017

The phrase "West Coast design" conjures an amplitude as generous as the American West. Broad balconies, cathedral ceilings, open floor plans, and the promise of—if not the reality of—deserts, groves, forests, or seashores beyond. West Coast design celebrates materials along a broad spectrum from wild to refined, and architects will incorporate boulders and trees they've found on-site just as soon as they'll import polished marble for the living-room hearth. West Coast design is glass and steel, but it's also bamboo and Douglas fir; it's industrial materials and woven fibers united by a palette that can be as vibrant as a Castillian cape or as sober as a Cistercian nave.

Architecturally, West Coast design offers residential architects a large menu of options to design in this mode, with lots of precedents to examine. There's Charles and Ray Eames's glass-and-steel Stahl House, the epitome of midcentury modernism that's perched on the same West Hollywood escarpment as Frank Lloyd Wright's textile-block Storer House—both homes synonymous with Los Angeles, despite the ubiquity of modernism or the otherworldliness of the Mayan revival. The stark white concrete blocks of Julia Morgan's Spanish colonial revival Hearst Castle share the same California coast as the graying redwood of Charles Moore's earthy but angular Sea Ranch. Moving up the coast into Oregon, Washington, and British Columbia, wood continues to be the dominant expression of nature employed by residential architects and designers—raw, refined, engineered, nailed, or fastened, and always nodding to the alders, cedars, firs, hemlocks, pines, and redwoods that are often within sight.

Bridge House, atop a 400-foot ridge that runs along
the western side of Denman Island in British Columbia

For architect Etienne de Villiers, it's both a virtue and a folly of West Coast design that the term can mean so much these days, thanks to the keyword tagging and algorithms of social media, where we all seem to find inspiration these days—including Villiers's clients.

Villiers is founder and principal of Etienne Design, based on Denman Island, about 100 miles west of Vancouver and part of the northern archipelago of Gulf Islands between mainland Canada and Vancouver Island. His projects along the Strait of Georgia are few but not far between—numbering ten within about 100 square miles, all united by a design approach that mixes the regional vernacular architectural traditions and a more contemporary use of renewable materials such as glue-laminated timber.

"We talk about West Coast design a lot in relation to custom homes, and, to me, that means stone fireplaces, timber roofs, and exposed timber tails, and posts and beams complemented by drywall. But at the end of the day, it's lots of windows," says Villiers, who reports that his client base is unusually open to innovation while also deeply interested in craftsmanship.

In 2011, two such clients came to him to design a home that could accommodate their growing family—the semiretired husband and wife had three adult sons, two of whom had partners of their own. They wanted to create something for their 160-acre tract of land they'd purchased on top of a 400-foot ridge that runs along the western side of Denman Island. Their plan was to commission a house on an 8-acre section as a family retreat and place to host friends, and Villiers designed what would be called the Bridge House, so called because of what's connected and what's revealed. The elevated living room and dining room act as a literal bridge between two bedroom wings, and by lifting that part of the structure, Villiers preserves the vista one catches when they arrive by foot or by car.

"We talk about West Coast design a lot in relation to custom homes, and, to me, that means stone fireplaces, timber roofs, and exposed timber tails, and posts and beams complimented by drywall. But at the end of the day, it's lots of windows," says the architect Etienne de Villiers.

"For me, the bridge was about the approach to the house, because, too often, a house blocks a view as you approach," says Villiers. "Here, when you arrive, you're looking under the house, so to speak—under the bridge—to see the view immediately and see the house in its context."

What makes the bridge possible are glulam beams, which create both uninterrupted views beneath the house as you climb to approach it and uninterrupted space in the bridge's main living area—preserving the vista and providing the kind of open-plan flexibility the owners wanted. Bridge House is clad in raw timber outside, which Villiers says weathers better than engineered wood in the damp Pacific Northwest (a hybrid approach he takes in his other residential projects). Inside, the Douglas fir glulam is exposed on nearly every surface and creates the effect of a honeyed glow at daybreak and sunset.

"Part of deciding on glulam as a strategy early on was freedom and experimentation," he says, "and it meant we could span large distances without massive timbers, which we needed for that bridge that was meant to facilitate the vista as you approach. It just made sense. It was a natural fit to use them in the main area, as well, and it became a design element that we could showcase inside."

Villiers worked with Island Timberframe and longtime collaborator Luc Trépanier, a Vancouver-based builder whom he calls "exceptionally talented" in his ability to work across the spectrum of glulam applications, from structural components to interior finish work. This is Villiers's fourth project with Island Timberframe, headquartered less than 15 miles away from Bridge House on Vancouver Island.

Initially, the Bridge House was meant to be a test case with the goal of building a larger house elsewhere on the property, after which the clients would eventually market the original house as a bed-and-breakfast. Fast forward to today, and, while the second, larger house (and the bed-and-breakfast) is on hold, Villiers and his associate designer, Jessica Booth, are creating an addition to the original home (which included a primary bedroom suite on one side of the bridge and guest suite on the other side). Booth's work on the addition calls for transforming some spaces to accommodate a home office and creating new ones to expand the number of bedrooms, as well as to create a little more autonomy for the guest suites with a separate entrance, laundry room, and kitchenette. The larger house—expanded and reconfigured—looks like an open "C" in plan, angled to maximize the views beyond.

And what about these vaunted views of the area that Villiers, Booth, and Trépanier worked to reveal? The lush green hills and deep-brown-black woodlands, dappled with fog and sunshine in equal measures—a coastal idyll as alluring as any in the West. Importantly, they have also revealed a more complicated history of deforestation that once powered industry but left the region poorer environmentally and culturally. More than 90 percent of the ancient forests of Vancouver Island have been logged, for instance, and new-growth forests are still catching up.

At Bridge House, the view is as much about what can be seen (and enjoyed) as it is about what we've forsaken—nearly at our peril.

"If you want to talk about 'West Coast design,' old-growth timber was very popular for a long time around here, but not any more. We are all acutely aware of its scarcity now," he says, "and I really think the future of sustainability is going to be renewable mass timber and recycled steel."

Builders—and architects—want to work with reliable products," says Villiers. "They want to work with things that won't twist and shrink. Things that will endure."

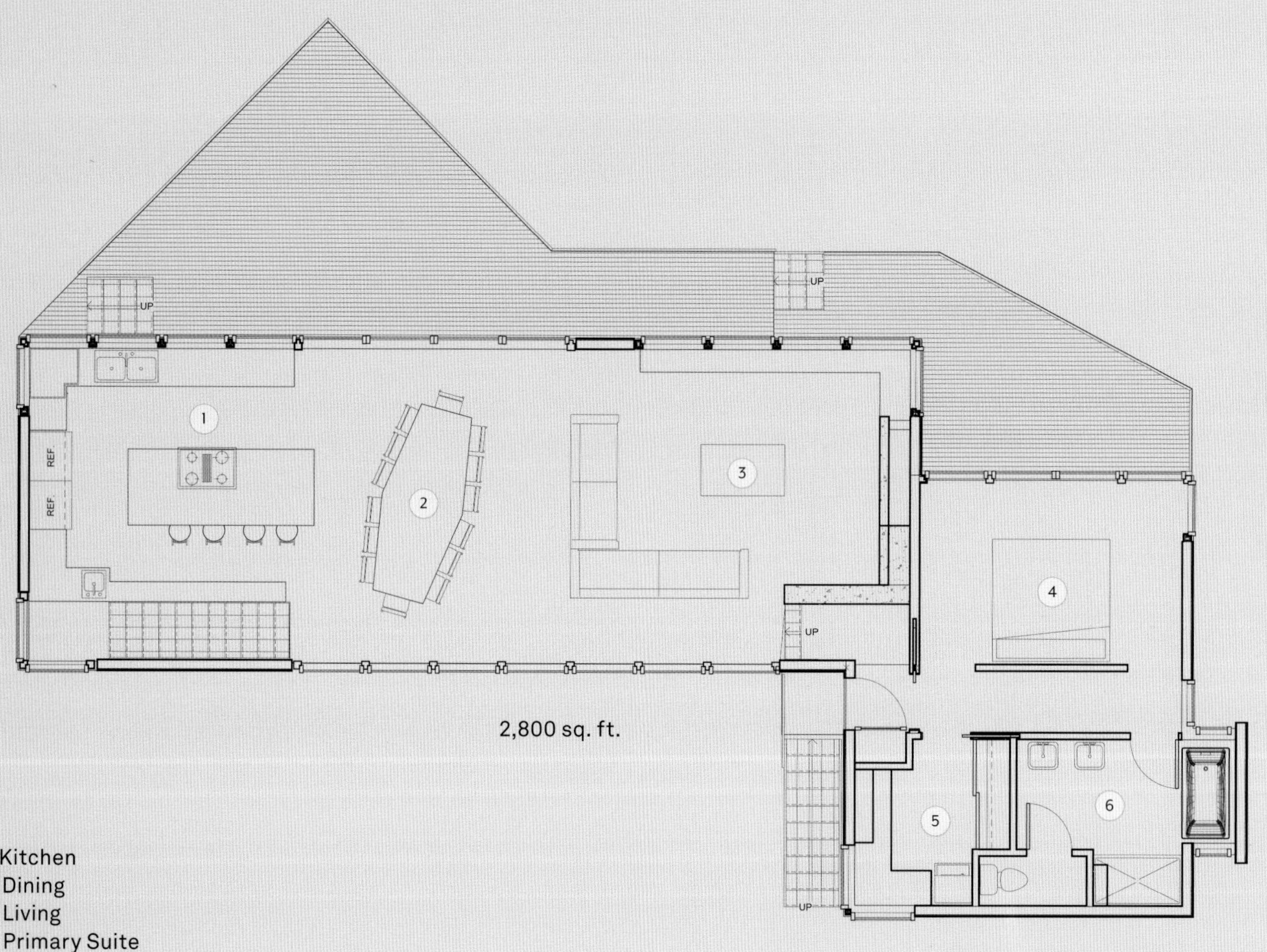

1 Kitchen
2 Dining
3 Living
4 Primary Suite
5 Laundry
6 Primary Bath

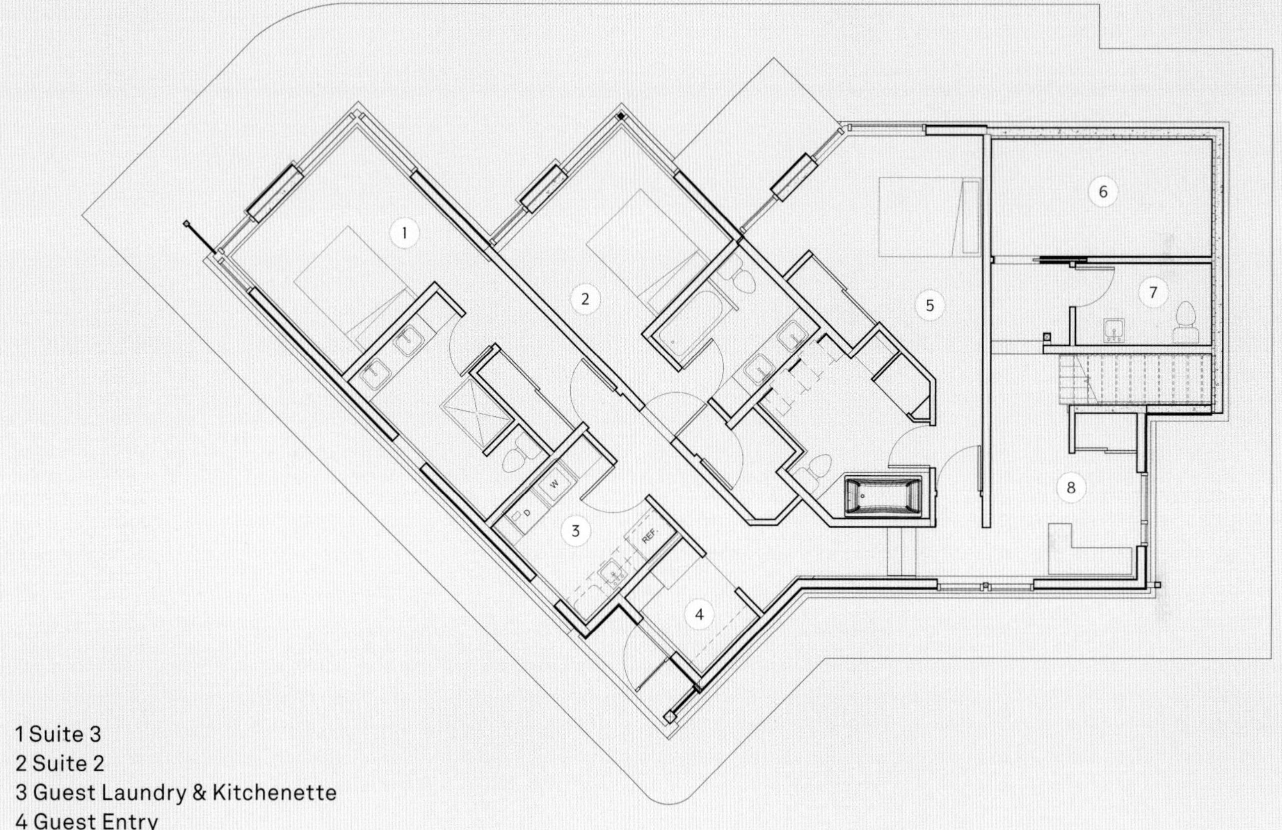

1 Suite 3
2 Suite 2
3 Guest Laundry & Kitchenette
4 Guest Entry
5 Suite 1
6 Mechanical Room
7 Powder
8 Main Entry

SPRUCE APARTMENTS

Barrett's Grove, London, England
Amin Taha / Groupwork
2015

The Spruce Apartments is the name of a five-story brick-clad building that stands on the same ridge as the A10 roadway—the nearby high street that traces an ancient Roman road and remains a major thoroughfare connecting a dozen London neighborhoods, including Dalston, Shoreditch, and Tottenham. Along Stoke Newington Road, as it is locally known, is a buzzy succession of storefronts that extend as far as the eye can see. But there's hardly time to find the vanishing point with Hackney carriages and the buses of four lines roaring by, and the heady mixture of exhaust, fried food, and hashish envelops the sidewalk, teeming with a steady stream of people ambling, dashing, darting, and chatting. An Afro-Caribbean market, an Ethiopian café, a Cuban taberna, a German doner kebab joint, a Turkish barber, a place called Gypsy Lust that sells prêt-à-porter shift dresses, and an outpost of the chain restaurant Nando's—the Dalston neighborhood offers everything to eat and see, and yet nothing for a visitor to declare by way of easy labels.

The wicker-woven balconies of London's Spruce Apartments offer enough outdoor space for two chairs and a table or, on hot nights, a family of three to sleep under the stars.

Off the A10 high street and extending both eastward and westward, row houses, ginnels, and low-slung industrial garages give way to Victorian- and Edwardian-era real estate developments marketed to workers who, more than a century ago, were attached to mill-related industries dotting the river Lea's delta. Today, these homes are targeted by Londoners looking to find their first or second rung on what's affectionately called the property ladder in UK design and real estate shows. The borough of Hackney, within which Dalson falls, has been seen as a post–Great Recession bellwether over the last decade, as property prices there also climbed the ladder—urged higher year after year by workers (and their families) in technology and creative industries, as well as finance. Observers have widely seen it as the best-performing borough in London, in fact, in light of the gains outgoing sellers made and the quick appreciation new buyers experienced. It's in this context that owner, developer, and architecture firm Groupwork designed the Spruce Apartments to attract couples and small families to an area that's

ideally situated about 2 miles from the touristy Circle Line to the southwest, the financial district to the south, and nearly 800 acres of combined green space in Victoria Park and Olympic Park to the west.

The Spruce is perched above much of the high street's activities on the north side of Barrett's Grove, and its residents enjoy a generous southern exposure overlooking the turrets, iron crestings, and terra-cotta finials of neighboring row houses. It's a narrow site, on which Groupwork founder and architect Amin Taha has stacked six apartments—two three-bedroom flats, three two-bedroom flats, and one one-bedroom flat. The form of the building is both familiar and peculiar for this part of town—it has a strong, gabled roof (as many of its neighbors do), but it's largely unadorned, in stark contrast to its neighbors, save for the wicker-woven balconies that jut out at regular intervals, whose counterpoints are the unornamented windows that puncture the façade, also at regular intervals.

Groupwork founder and the project's architect Amin Taha uses brick as a skin over the CLT superstructure to provide ventilation and a rain screen.

One's first impression on approaching it, aside from its form, is its façade, composed of red bricks arranged in an open stretcher bond, meaning the bricks have regular gaps in them rather than a closed stretcher bond with staggered vertical joints. In this way, Taha uses the brickwork as less of a structural strategy and more of a skin over the CLT super-structure of the building, which provides non-load-bearing ventilation and a rain screen. It's a skin that also helps Taha and his design team create a relationship to the burgundy brickwork of the adjacent Edwardian-era school that wraps around the eastern and northern flanks of the property.

The prefabricated CLT panels used throughout the project as a superstructure support walls, floors, and the roof. On the outside, it's been treated with an intumescent varnish, which acts as an insulating barrier and fire protection, then was clad in black landscape fabric—deepening our impression of texture along the façade as red against black, in contrast to other buildings on the block, whose red bricks are joined with buff-, tan-, and cream-colored mortars.

The Spruce occupies a narrow site, on which architect Amin Taha stacked six apartments in a way that's both familiar and peculiar for this part of town—it has a strong, gabled roof (as many of its neighbors do), but it's largely unadorned, in stark contrast to its neighbors.

On the inside, Taha does not conceal the superstructure and leaves it unadorned. The CLT panels farthest from the windows have retained their original, slightly golden hues, while the ones closest to the windows have lightened with the sun. Especially on the upper floors, the building's southern exposure kicks up stunning sunsets, and the honeyed glow of the front living room and kitchen is amplified by the warmth of the CLT panels no matter their coloration.

Taha's shotgun-style flats open midhall off a skylit stairwell shared by the building's residents. Each landing has been subtly personalized, each threshold framed by castoff sneakers or shoes. Entering a typical flat, if you look to the right, you'll see the bedrooms. If you look to the left, you'll see the living room and kitchen. That's the basic layout. The ground-floor unit flips the program and, uniquely, has a private courtyard off the back, in lieu of the balcony the upper floors enjoy. All the flats are one level except for the penthouse, which is owned by Ben Cox and his family and uniquely includes two floors connected via private staircase, also midhall. Cox admires the building's form and the architect Taha's intentions—downstairs is an arrangement typical of the building, with two bedrooms (one of which the penthouse's owners have converted into a guest room and occasional workspace, and one of which is their daughter's bedroom). Upstairs is the primary bedroom, with vaulted ceiling to the back and a mezzanine to the front that the couple uses as a home office, overlooking the living and dining area below.

"When we bought this house, we didn't expect to be working at home full time, and we didn't expect to have a child. Then we got pregnant. Then the pandemic happened, and this house has been able to take it. All of it," says Cox.

In all the flats, two rooms to the rear can be
adapted for sleeping, work, or play against the
warm tones of the Edwardian-era school buildings
that encircle the site to the north and east.

He also describes some of the quirks of the project. As the building has settled, the CLT panels have split in places in a way that's apparent if you're looking for it, but otherwise imperceptible to the casual gaze. Spruce sap, still tacky to the touch, oozes out of the ceiling in places. The insulated CLT panels are so effective that, in winter, the Coxes have hardly ever used the in-floor heating (and, for several summers, there has been more than one night they've elected to sleep on their balcony to beat the heat). As a result of the prefabricated construction, the wet-room shower on the main floor of their apartment doesn't drain quite as well as they'd like. Still, he says, the bones of the building and the lines of sight, as conceived by the design team, are well considered—and the progressive use of CLT matches what he calls the "design-conscious and creatively progressive area" of Dalston and environs.

"It is a fully lived-in house and we use every square foot of it, so it doesn't look like it did when we bought it, but the design, itself, remains a strong foundation for the life we've created here," says Cox.

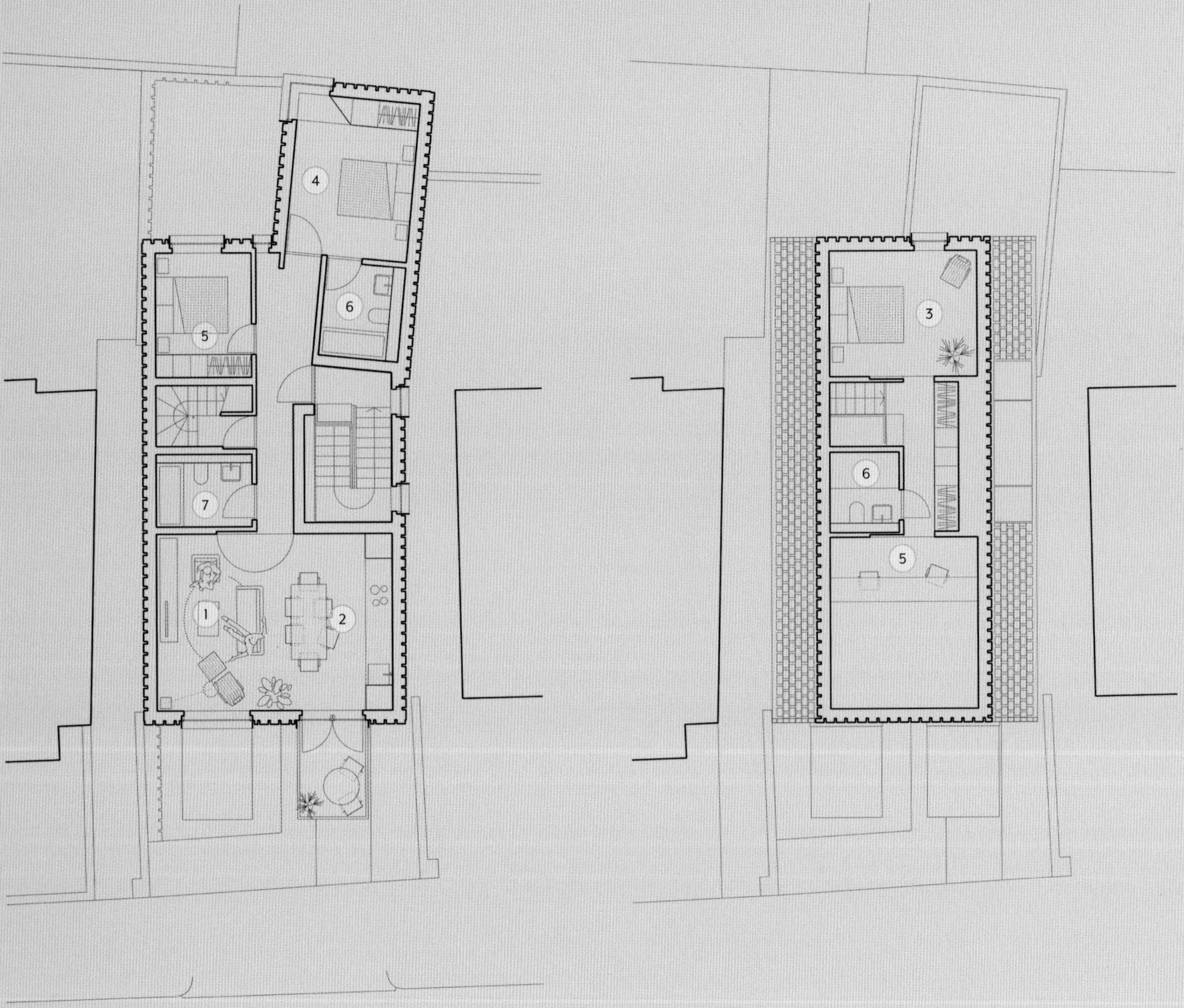

1 Living Room
2 Kitchen
3 Primary Bedroom
4 Bedroom 2
5 Bedroom 3 / Study
6 En Suite
7 Bathroom
8 Entry Lobby

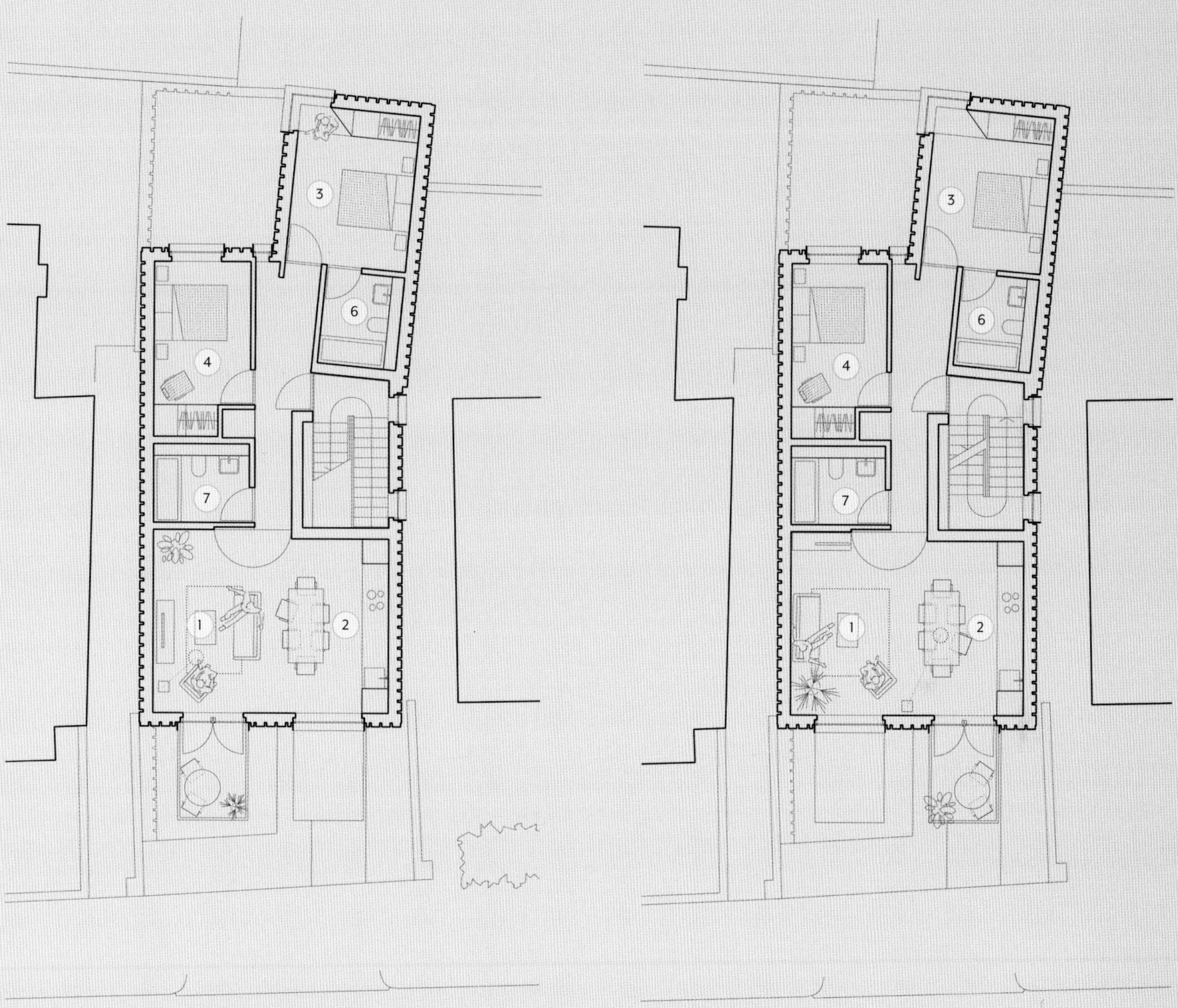

1 Living Room
2 Kitchen
3 Primary Bedroom
4 Bedroom 2
5 Bedroom 3 / Study
6 En Suite
7 Bathroom
8 Entry Lobby

HAUS H

Vienna, Austria
Veit Pedit
2019

The economic fallout of World War I recalibrated life for millions of Austrians, whose food and housing shortages were exacerbated by the arrival of more than 300,000 repatriated refugees in 1918 and 1919. Thousands of Viennese pushed westward into a piedmont of the distant Alps to create subsistence settlements in the Vienna Woods of self-built wooden shacks and fruit and vegetable patches. Eventually, these "wild settlers" formed cooperative associations to qualify for financial support from Vienna's municipal government, and the city's newly formed Settlement Office began designating land in 1921 for planned communities on the Garden City model of self-sufficiency, with zones for agriculture and homes. At Friedensstadt, Hermeswiese, Heuberg, and Rosenhügel, the Settlement Office's effort kick-started the largest social housing program of any European city to design and construct single-family homes, as well as large multifamily and mixed-use developments at the scale of the city block, interspersed with public amenities, kitchen and communal gardens, and parks.

The rear garden from the site's initial Loos/ Schütte-Lihotzky scheme has been replaced by a lush lawn and small biopool. A tensile structure that supports an retractable awning extends over the balcony, and it also extends the geometry of the saltbox form.

From 1921 to 1924, the Settlement Office's nearly two hundred architects were overseen by its first architectural director, Adolf Loos, one of the high priests of modernism, who influenced modern debates about architectural ornament, craft, labor, and the function of interior spaces. Across his built work, essays, lectures, and polemical positions, Loos believed that an economy of means is a meaningful strategy to create space.

This belief wasn't about money, per se (since he certainly enjoyed healthy construction budgets with some of his clients over his thirty-year career), but about creating an architectural language that valued spareness over wastefulness. Façades should be unornamented, saving craftspeople precious time and energy and saving a building from appearing dated too quickly. Interior spaces should be proportionate to their function—for cooking, for sleeping, for gathering—instead of being a function of convention—kitchen, bedroom, salon. In this way, he was ideally suited to oversee a mass-housing campaign for a Social Democratic government.

Among the Settlement Office's first efforts, Heuberg was planned by Loos and the architect Margarete Schütte-Lihotzky to offer a series of attached dwellings types on long, narrow plots with gardens in the rear. Residents committed to three thousand hours of work to build their own homes, the plans of which were rudimentary and relatively easy to carry out. Over the years, and as these settlement communities went from representing economic and social frontiers to serving as retreats for urbanites, many of the homes in Heuberg have been adapted, renovated, and expanded. Some of the gardens remain in shape only, having been converted to patios. Others remain alive as patches of manicured grass.

When a family of three approached the Vienna-based architect Veit Pedit in 2013 to help them reimagine a trapezoidal site they'd purchased in Heuberg, Pedit counseled them to abandon the house plans that came with the land. A year and a half later, and after engaging another firm that specializes in prefabricated homes, they returned to Pedit, who went on to design what would become Haus H for them. Completed in 2019, it's a straightforward saltbox form with a simple gabled roof whose pregrayed, irregularly wide larch board cladding the exterior makes the home a subdued contribution to the neighborhood. Its appearance might also make it a perfect candidate for Cape Cod's Santuit, Florida's Seaside, or Sonoma's Sea Ranch. Yet, as familiar as Haus H seems, Pedit's design is laser-focused on evoking the modernist history of the site.

Veit Pedit designed a straightforward saltbox form with a simple gabled roof whose pregrayed, irregularly wide larch board cladding the exterior makes the home a subdued contribution to the neighborhood. It was completed in 2019.

"From an urban point of view, we are still in Vienna, but it feels like the countryside. Function and place and reaction to neighborhood—all of the ways we define context," he says, "is part of the process of finding variations that will lead to a final design. I think I am trying to make a new start with every project somehow. Of course it is all designed in an architectural language, but it is always a new start."

In the historic garden settlements of Vienna, city ordinances govern things such as the front façade and the degree to which you can remake the home. Haus H's Heuberg is outside that zone (hence the irregularly shaped lot), but as Pedit notes, the city is still keen to preserve the 80-square-meter footprint (or about 861 square feet) of the original structures as a limit for new construction. The city's height limit of 5.5 meters (about 18 feet) was also tricky for Pedit, owing to the grade change on the site, which allowed him to use 5.5 meters as an average rather than a maximum. But the gabled roof does not count as part of that height regulation, "so the extra room is like a gift above," he says.

To keep the scale and massing of the home in compliance, Pedit dug down into the hillside to bury a third of the house underground. In total, three stories and three mezzanines, which count for six levels and about 1,884 square feet, belie the home's outward modesty. The rear garden has been replaced by a lush lawn and small biopool (sans chlorine). A tensile structure that supports a retractable awning extends over the balcony, and it also extends the geometry of the saltbox form in a slight nod to deconstructivism.

In the mid-1990s, Pedit apprenticed with fellow Austrian Mark Mack in Venice Beach, California, soaking up the Los Angeles area's heady mixture of design theory and what one scholar called "the architecture and urban design of nontradition." After moving back to Vienna in 1996, he designed his first house for clients Hemma and Börge Schichl, the form of which would have been right at home in Venice or even Malibu, but whose primary material—in a decidedly traditional mode—was wood. His colleagues groused at wood's poor ability to create thermal comfort in the subarctic climate zone of Gratkorn, a suburb of Graz.

Pedit knew better—and proved them wrong—and for twenty-five years through his firm Pedit & Partner Architects, he has completed more than fifty projects that incorporate timber. Today, he says, CLT is preferable to timber, especially in Austria, which manufactures a lot of the mass timber products for the global market, making it the most economic choice for his local clients.

Heuberg is a community planned by the architects Adolf Loos and Margarete Schütte-Lihotzky to offer a series of attached dwelling types on long, narrow plots with gardens in the rear.

Aside from the tensile space frame, the balcony of Haus H announces that it might be slightly different from its neighbors in both form and material. Composed of cross-laminated spruce timber, it offers a key to passersby that this house is more than meets the eye. One can see upon entering that the 10 cm thick walls have no cladding and that the CLT is left exposed (albeit coated for protection), and Pedit used CLT for the ceiling and the roof, which is divided into two large panels. Wood, says Pedit, is better for homeowners in the long run—especially if you maintain and treat it well—and it retains heat from the geothermal well, especially when paired with triple-pane windows.

"I like to build with wood—for its haptic nature of wood, but also because wood is natural, it's good to work with, and it finishes well too," says Pedit. "I don't make a religion out of wood—I like stone and concrete too—but I think it is a nice material to live in."

"I like to build with wood—for its haptic nature of wood, but also because wood is natural, it's good to work with, and it finishes well too," says Pedit. "I don't make a religion out of wood—I like stone and concrete too—but I think it is a nice material to live in."

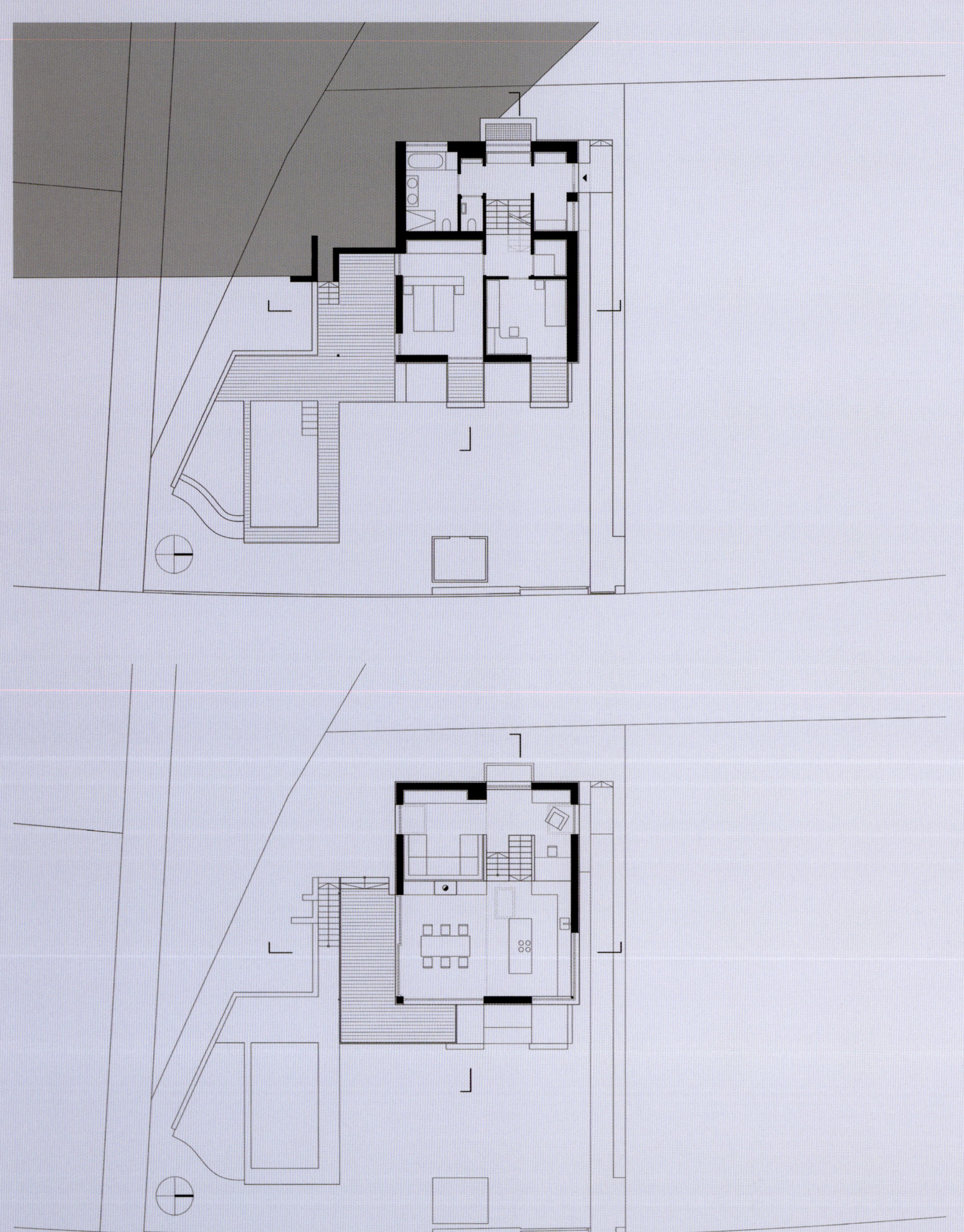

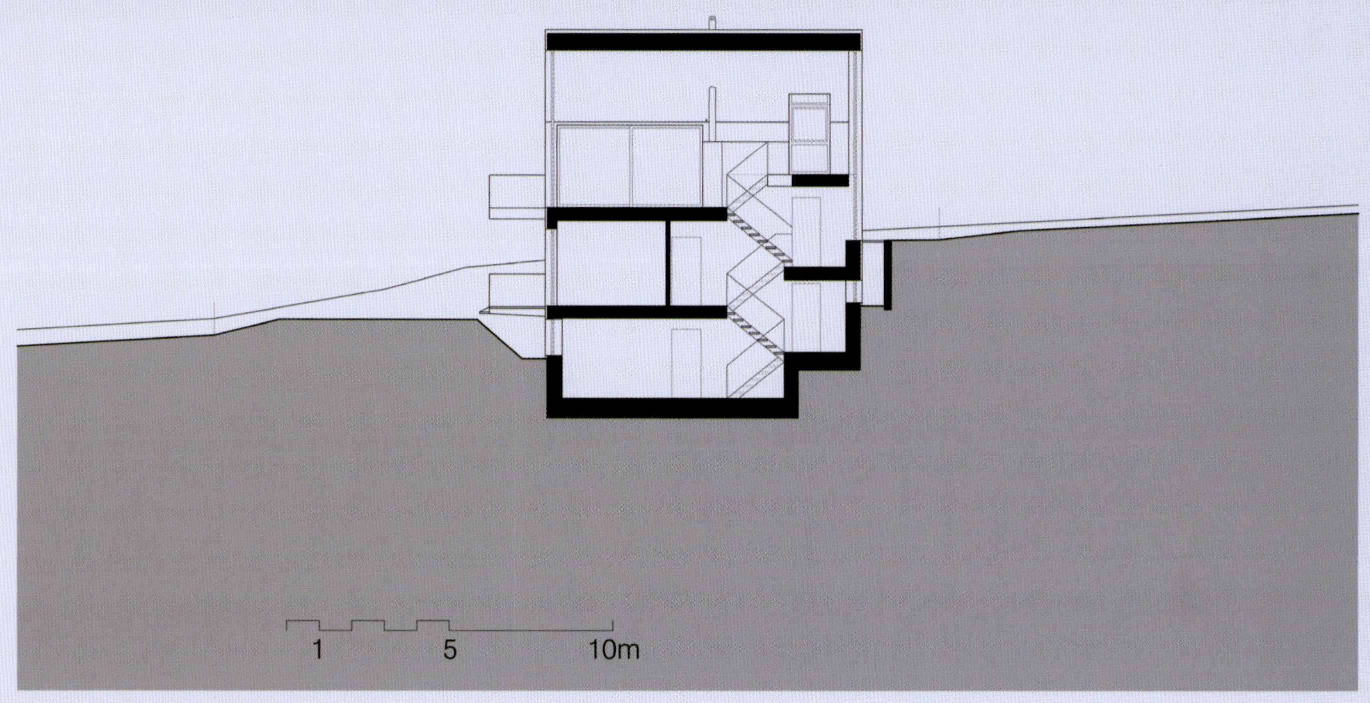

1   5   10m

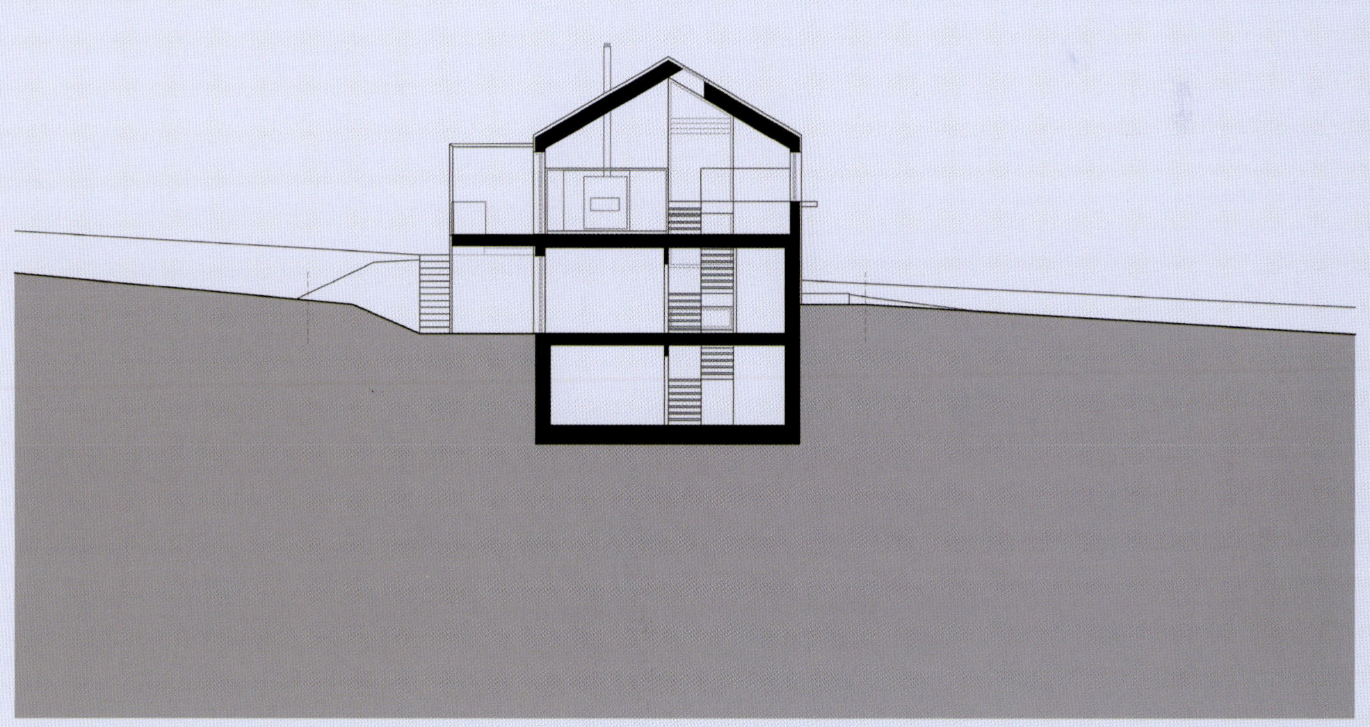

CLT HOUSE

Fiona Dunin, founder and director of her eponymous architecture firm, showcases the load-bearing capacity of cross-laminated timber by creating a second-story bridge that connects two halves of Melbourne's 6,027-square-foot CLT House. She also casts us back to the pre-Victorian factories in the north of England, which utilized the sawtooth roof as a strategy to admit light and ventilate large spaces. She translates both of these forms borrowed from civil engineering to enrich and, indeed, support the thrum of home in the throes of projects and progeny. CLT House is nothing if not a machine for living that's both simple and complex.

The architect Louis Kahn once urged us to ask a brick what it wants to be, and the brick, he said, would naturally reply, "An arch." The same logic holds for wood products engineered to span great distances. What does wood want to be? A tree, again, perhaps, upon which architects may realize their ambitions. But Dunin goes beyond bridges and boughs at CLT House to explore how typologies can collide to create spaces that are daring in their volume and refined in their finishes, as well as luminous as any factory by incorporating a sawtooth roof—the project's leitmotif.

The architect Fiona Dunin goes beyond bridges and boughs at CLT House to explore how typolocies can collide to create spaces that are daring in their volumes and refined in their finishes.

Dunin completed CLT House in 2019 just outside Melbourne in Victoria, the southeasternmost state, where a lot of mass timber activity has been focused over the last decade due, in part, to XLam Australia opening a factory about three hours north of the city. In 2022, the Australian government launched a $300 million timber-building program to encourage uptake of cross-laminated timber and glued-laminated timber by financing eligible projects in the commercial, industrial, healthcare, education, and multifamily sectors. The boost comes at a time when three mass timber towers are underway—one in Melbourne, one in Sydney, and one in Perth—totaling 104 stories and $1.9 billion in investment and including timber products imported from Austria, Germany, and Italy.

Dunin's single-family home is a counterpoint to those developments in scale, but also in spirit—and served as a proving ground for CLT that her clients, infrastructure developers who work on large-scale projects abroad, wanted to explore. "He wanted to test CLT and glulam so he could use it on his larger projects later, and he really wanted to understand mass timber," says Dunin, "so it was a great opportunity for me to experiment with it and see how it would work at a residential level."

The other broad criterion was family. Her client has several adult children, along with their partners and grandchildren, and wanted a house that could accommodate everyone. To meet the brief, she renovated a 1970s ranch-style house by insulating the brickwork by replacing the single-pane windows with double-pane windows, and giving it a new lease of life. That structure remains as the first floor, painted with a lime wash to give the brick a milky hue on the outside, and redesigned to include five bedrooms on the inside. She added a pavilion to the northwest, which serves as a bunk room for the grandkids (offering their visiting parents a much-needed chance to sleep in). The second level of the home is essentially a bridge that spans a porte cochère below and connects the older main house below with the pavilion beyond, and it contains the clients' primary suite, terrace, library, and guest suite. Since the project was completed in 2019, the bridge, which centers on a library, also ended up accommodating the clients' business as well, during the pandemic-era lockdowns.

To meet the brief, Dunin renovated a 1970s ranch-style house, giving it a new lease of life. That structure remains as the first floor, painted with a lime wash.

The house is as luminous as any factory that utilizes a sawtooth roof, and Dunin created a library and workspace that bridges two parts of the expanded house.

Besides being a flexible space on the inside, the bridge is also the most distinctive feature of the home on the outside. Glulam beams support the CLT panels above and the forms of Dunin's syncopated sawtooth roof and offer a high-relief cadence for the eye to follow along the south and north elevations. Below the ridgelines of the roof, the downward slopes are fitted with photovoltaic panels, and the bridge was devised as a series of identical modular sections by Dunin, who reports that the CLT elements of the building went up in less than a week, and the on-site installation crew found efficiencies in its composition and form. "Once you do one module and one sawtooth section, you can do ten more easily," she says.

Inside, light is admitted by the roof's flanks, which run the length of the library as a clerestory array might in a nave, and open to flue the space and promote natural ventilation in winter and summer. Norwegian spruce CLT panels produced by Stora Enso are left exposed and are finished with a nearly clear lime wash, while Radiata (or Monterey) pine produced by XLam Australia creates the floor beneath, all supported with glulam posts and beams.

The project's owner explicitly asked Dunin
to experient with mass timber. The other
broad criterion? Family. Her client has several
adult children, along with their partners
and grandchildren, and wanted a house
that could accommodate everyone.

"The space is big and feels almost monastic in its simplicity, and you can see all the CLT and exposed screws that are beautifully done," says Dunin, who thinks she'll continue to work with CLT, especially since the Australian market continues to favor it, and especially since it has so much to offer urban and rural circumstances where prefabrication makes sense, either for efficiency's sake or for geographical reasons.

"We're doing a project in Tasmania on a remote island, and everything comes across by ferry anyway, so prefabrication and modular construction is already our starting point there, and we'll use glulam for that one," she says, "but I'd love to work with mass timber more, especially as more engineers start working with it too, making it more viable."

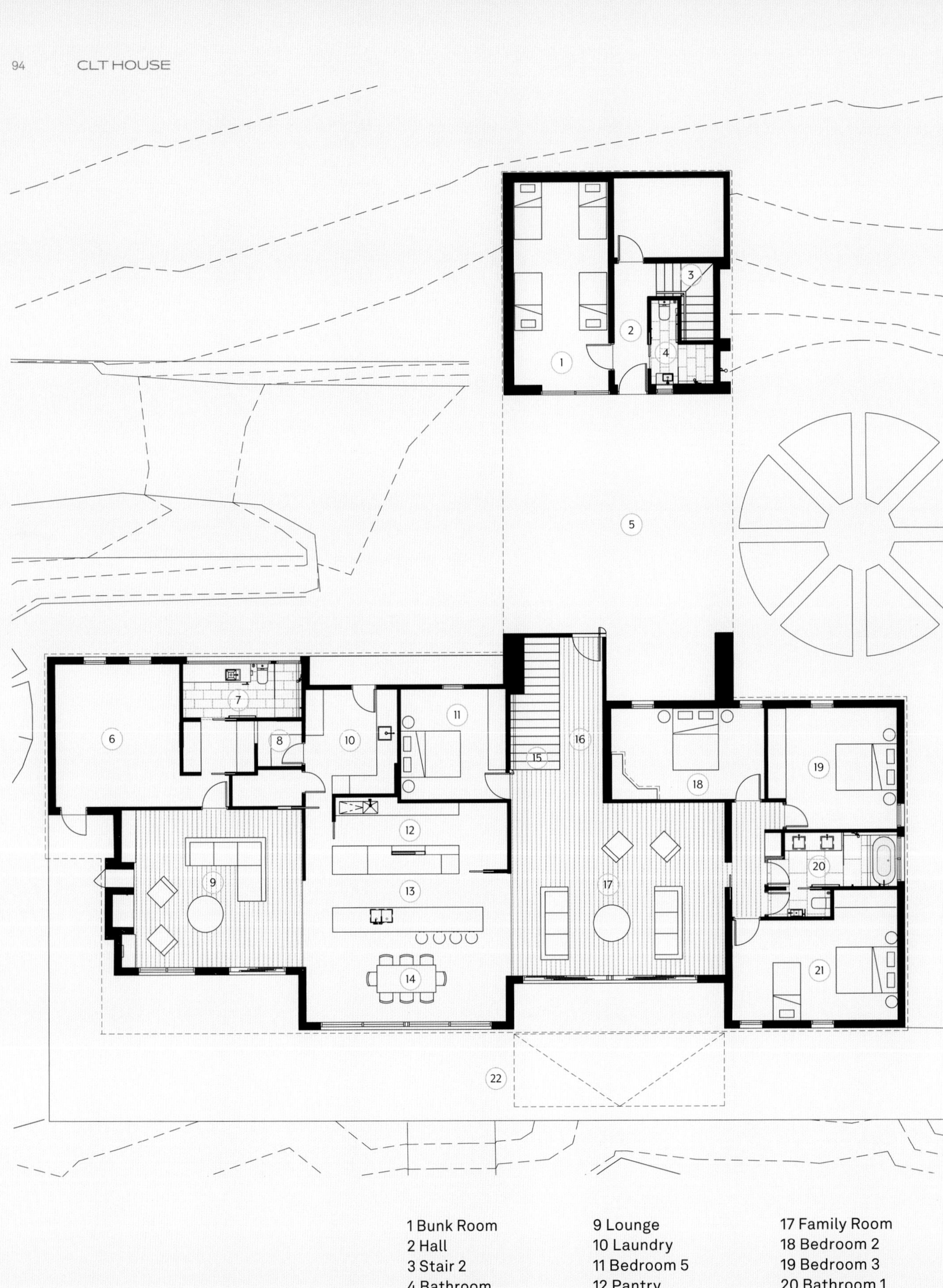

1 Bunk Room
2 Hall
3 Stair 2
4 Bathroom
5 Carport
6 Bedroom 1
7 En Suite 1
8 Linen Closet
9 Lounge
10 Laundry
11 Bedroom 5
12 Pantry
13 Kitchen
14 Dining
15 Stair 1
16 Entry
17 Family Room
18 Bedroom 2
19 Bedroom 3
20 Bathroom 1
21 Bedroom 4
22 Terrace
0 1 2 3 5

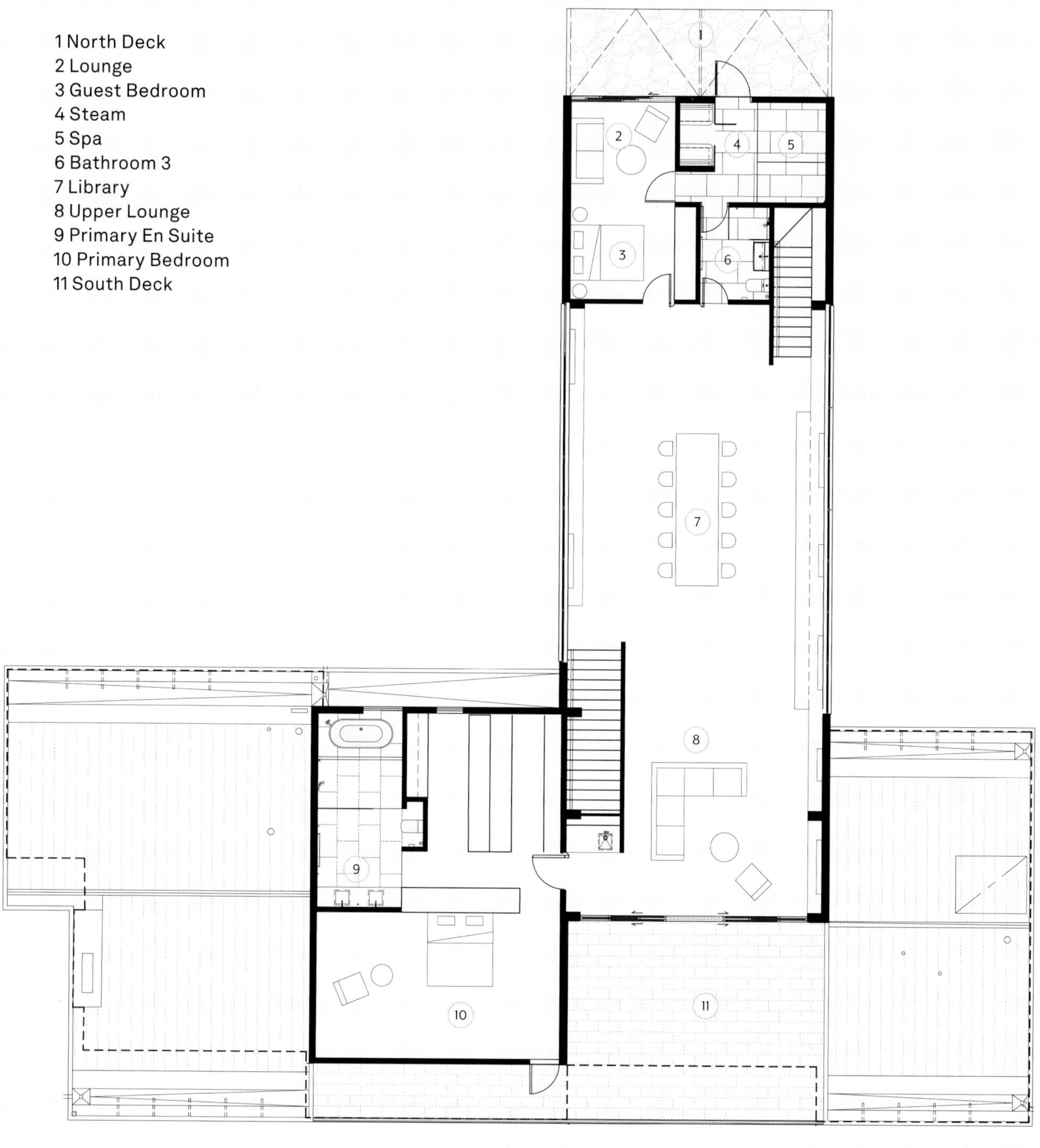

1 North Deck
2 Lounge
3 Guest Bedroom
4 Steam
5 Spa
6 Bathroom 3
7 Library
8 Upper Lounge
9 Primary En Suite
10 Primary Bedroom
11 South Deck
0 1 2 3 5

CLT HOUSE

**Seattle, Washington, USA
atelierjones
2015**

In architecture's popular media, Seattle's CLT House has been called a wooden "wonder" and the product of "a love affair with wood"—breathless encomiums that happen to be, in this case, well deserved, to celebrate the first single-family home in the United States to be constructed entirely of cross-laminated timber. Yet, its own architect and owner, Susan Jones, prefers to call it a "modest 1,500-square-foot single-family home," which is about 25 percent smaller than the average American home and is situated on a compact triangular lot across from an alley and parking lot.

The truth about CLT House, then, seems to be somewhere in the middle. It is, indeed, a north star for mass timber's architects and builders, and Jones's modesty certainly belies that importance. But the real story in the middle goes beyond a showcase for what's possible at the single-family residential scale and, therefore, possible at larger scales. It's also a story about a deeply personal project for Jones and her family that was designed in the aftershocks of the Great Recession and during what she calls "lots of late, dark nights." Her goal during those nights of sketching and model making might have seemed simple enough at first: to make something for a growing family in a sustainable way during a global financial crisis. But the goalposts shifted when Jones committed to making an entire home composed of a relatively new material on the market that had more detractors than advocates, despite its promise for decarbonization and renewable material pipelines.

The exterior of CLT House is wrapped in Rockwool insulation, helping it achieve an R-38 exterior wall rating, and then clad in 1 × 4 in. Douglas fir planks from Montana Timber Products, precharred as a sealing and preserving method.

"To put it into context, we had to move—we were in a condo-
minium since I was a graduate student that was 1,000 square
feet, and I started to have kids when I was thirty-six, and
while we could make it work at first, we just needed more
space. The kids wanted privacy. I wanted privacy. So, it became
clear that I needed to build something for the family we were
becoming," she says. "I was a client, yes, but I also used this as
a chance to take an ethical position about the profession."

After seeing homes that seemed to be made of plywood in
an Austrian catalog around 2011, Jones began digging into
their designs and materials and discovered they were actually made of cross-laminated timber. She began investigat-
ing logistics. At the time, Austria was the top exporter of
mass timber products to European architects and builders. If
anyone in the US was looking to work with glulam or CLT in
2011, Austria would have also been a top choice on the East
Coast, mixed in with some Canadian sources. Jones sourced
hers from Structurlam's plant in Penticton, British Columbia,
which was on the right side of the country for her (and only a
five-hour truck drive away from Seattle).

On-site, the sixty-seven CLT panels went up in just twelve days, hewn from the timber of twenty trees, which were replaced in nature by planting another twenty trees. Most of the interior features the gently whitewashed but largely unfinished panels—save for the kitchen, which uses drywall in a concession to building codes. The exterior is wrapped in Rockwool insulation, helping it achieve an R-38 exterior wall rating, and then clad in 1 × 4 in. Douglas fir planks from Montana Timber Products, precharred as a sealing and preserving method (called yakisugi in Japan, or shou-sugi-ban in the US), which boosts its fire resistance. The charred Douglas fir also softens the decidedly modernist home for a neighborhood once dominated by beach cabins, which today has an eclectic feel after successive waves of postwar single-family homes went up—some are bungalows bearing cedar shingles, some are traditional saltboxes that still approximate their original size and scale, and some are split-levels that could be Anywhere, USA. Jones aimed to cut through all of that and express something that is regional in its form and appearance for beachside communities in Cascadia. To wit, the *Seattle Times* even called CLT House an "urban beach cabin" in a 2016 profile, which offers at least one measure of success in terms of contextuality.

This is a story about a pioneering use of mass timber at the single-family residential scale. It's also a story about a deeply personal project for Jones and her family that was designed in the aftershocks of the Great Recession and during what she calls "lots of late, dark nights."

Passersby might stop to look a little longer at CLT House because of its handsomely charred façade of mottled blacks, browns, and grays, and its deeply inset windows that showcase the thickness of the structural panels. They might also notice the rhombic pitch of the roof, which appears especially dramatic by the eave line's notched base concealing a gutter that would otherwise be visible on a conventionally appointed house. In plan, Jones drew the house to mimic the acute triangle of the lot. Along the triangle's hypotenuse, where you might have expected a shear alley wall, Jones notches out a vertical, ground-to-roof light well for the interior at the midpoint. She also notches out a carport at the rear, sheltered by what appears to be the lost eave from the façade.

"On the outside, they see a triangle," says Jones, "and when they come in—we had 1,500 people tour it over the first few years—they see that this is an experimental house. Most of them say, 'I love this house and I'm bringing my friends to see it,' and others say, 'I want to understand it better—and they ask me, 'So, what is CLT?'"

As a neighbor, Jones has offered a demonstration piece. As an architect, she's offered a prototype—not just for single-family homes nationwide, but also in her own push to create affordable homes for the economic "missing middle" of Americans. Her eight-story, 126-unit multifamily project, called Heartwood, opened in 2023 in Seattle's Capitol Hill neighborhood for residents earning 60 to 100 percent of the area household median income. It's the first Type IV-C building in America (or heavy timber construction, per the model International Building Code), and while it might not be the equivalent of three dozen "CLT Houses," it encapsulates everything Jones learned in making a home for her family.

"CLT puts the designer in the driver's seat of production—we do the drawings in the office, we sign the BIM drawings, we send them off, they're cut, they show up on a flatbed truck—and if they don't go together on-site, then there is only one person to blame: me, Susan," she says. "Embracing that risk, then, is something I can't emphasize enough as the challenge and the reward."

NORTH ELEVATION

SOUTH ELEVATION

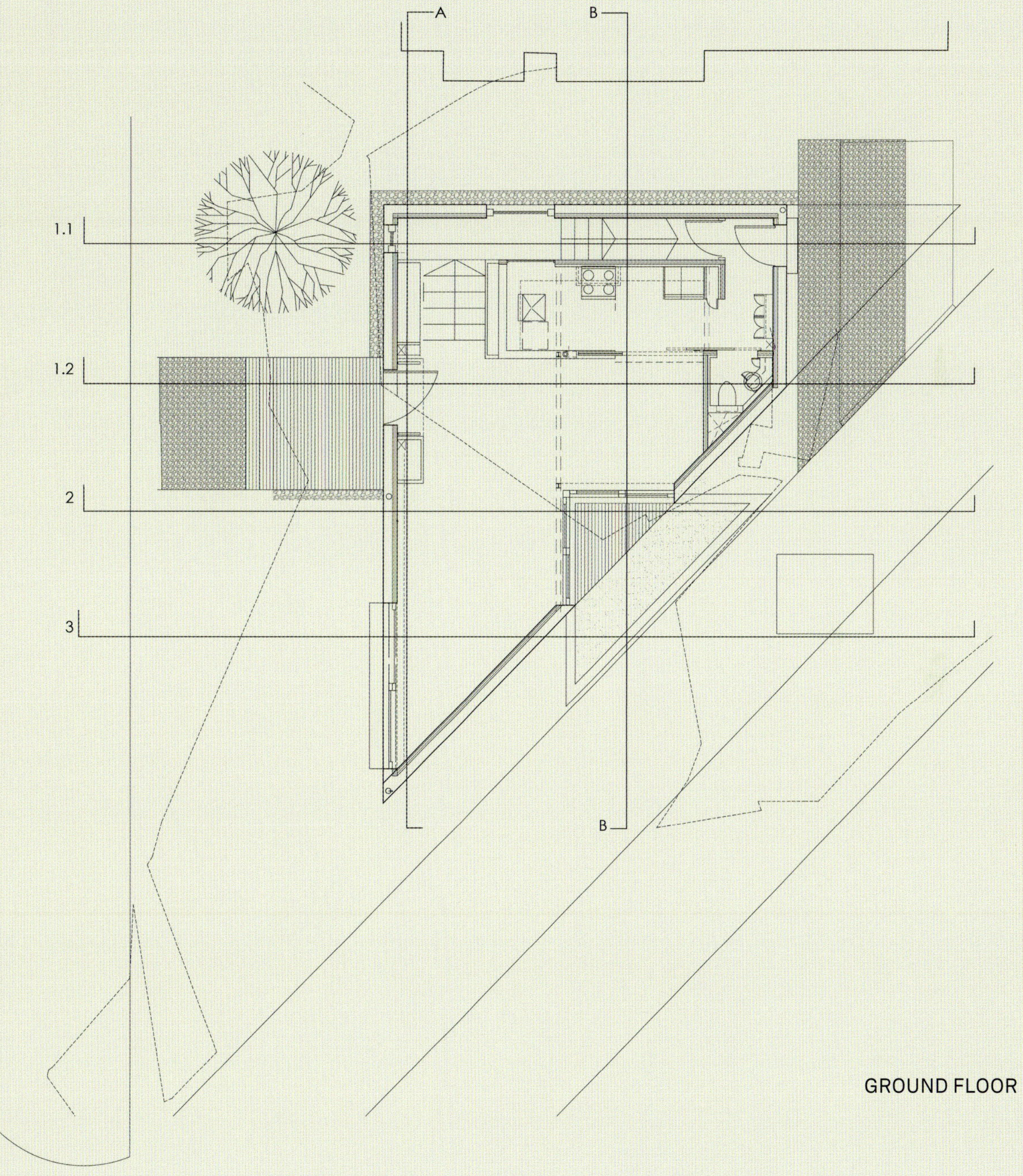

GROUND FLOOR

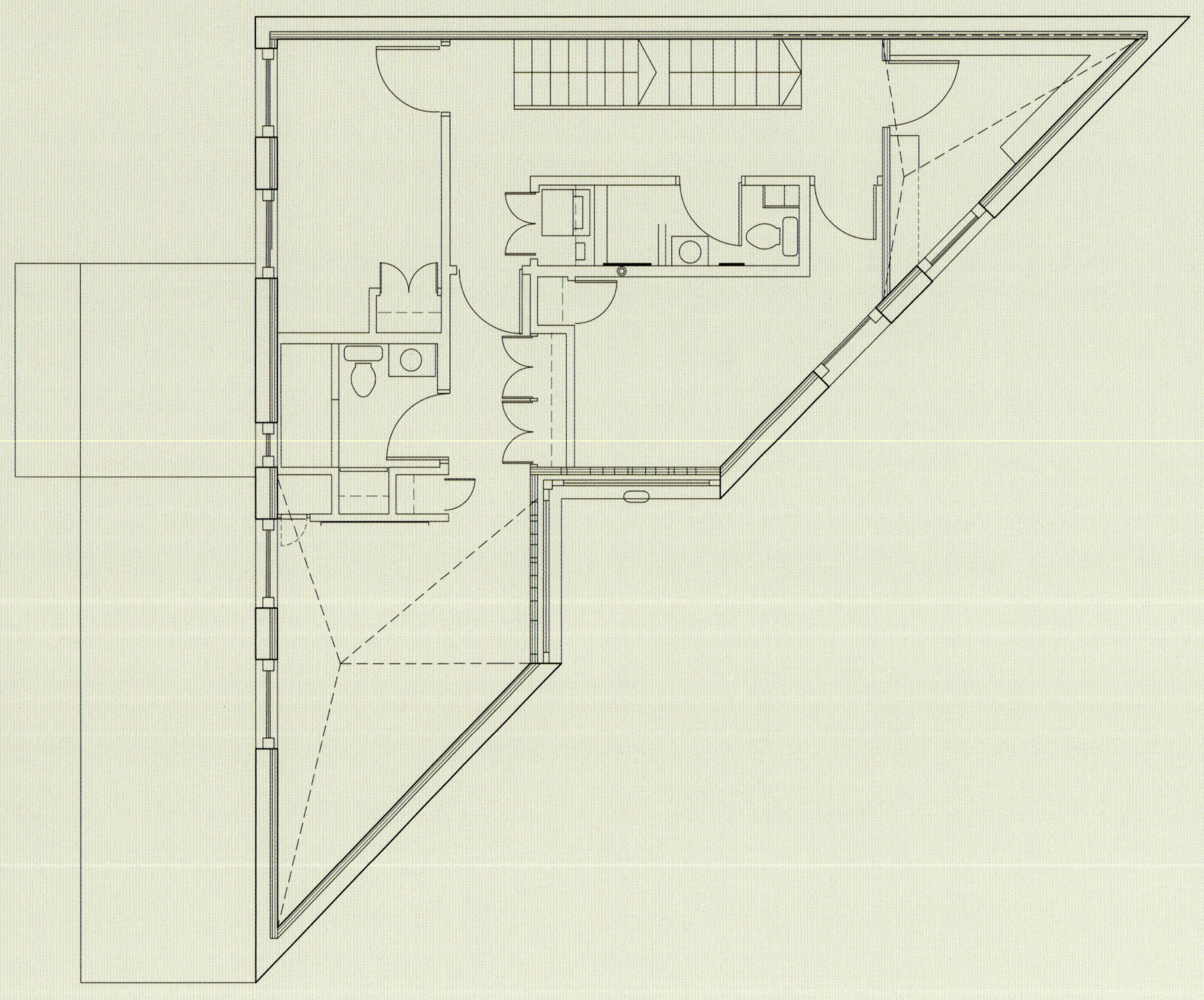

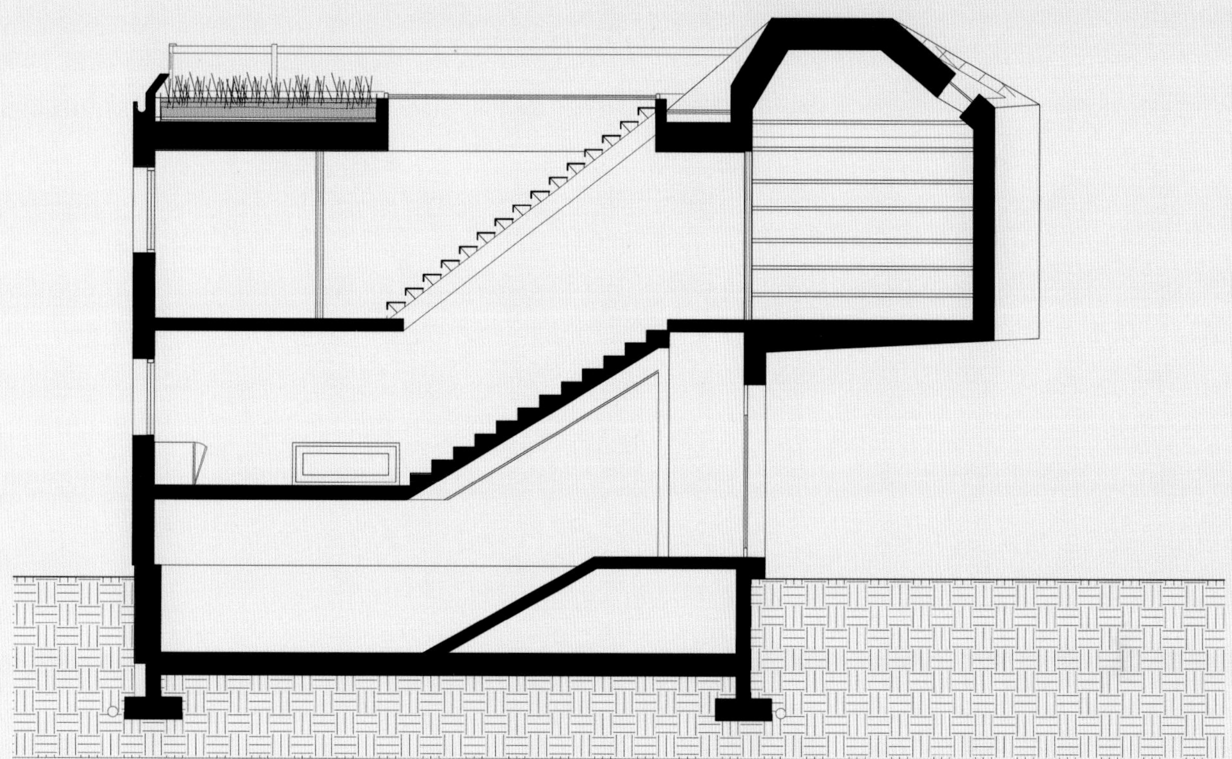

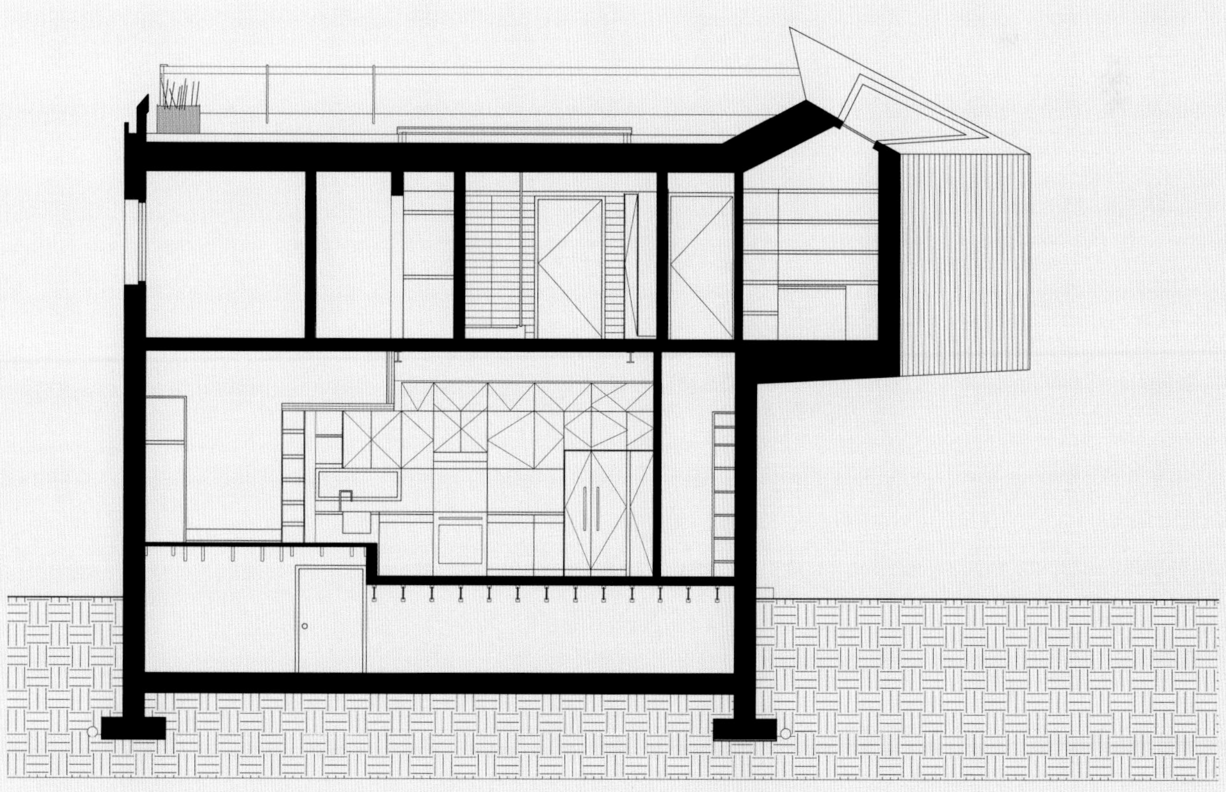

HOUTEN HERENHUIS

Amsterdam, Netherlands
Lidewij Lenders (Maatworks)
2010

Houten Herenhuis, or the "Pinewood House," is the first CLT and glulam house to be built in Amsterdam and possibly the first in the Netherlands. It's quintessentially Dutch in all but material, occupying a sliver of real estate with narrow frontage and multiple levels connected by a staircase that pulls triple duty as circulation, sculpture, and unprogrammed space for just about anything. The entrance and sleeping spaces occupy the lower two floors, and the living room, dining room, and rooftop terrace occupy the top two floors, closest to the light and possessing enviable views of the eastern harbor of Amsterdam. The clients—a couple—wanted a place that had lots of open floor space in spite of the decidedly narrow profile of the lot and squeezed, vertical orientation of the house. One of them had also lived in a timber house in Sweden before moving to Amsterdam and wanted to translate that experience to a city whose building traditions are masonry and concrete and to a country that isn't exactly known for a surfeit of trees. That was the design brief for Lidewij Lenders, principal architect of Amsterdam-based Maatworks, a firm that has done a lot with mass timber since Houten Herenhuis' completion in 2010 and whose philosophy has been shaped, in many ways, by what she learned working on this project.

Houten Herenhuis, designed by Maatworks, is part of a new development that mimics the scale of the canal houses built between the fifteenth and nineteenth centuries.

Houten Herenhuis is located on Steigereiland, the northern-most island of Ijburg, an ex novo neighborhood created with artificial islands in the mid-1990s on the basis of plans initially devised in the mid-1960s by the architects Jo van den Broek and Jacob Bakema. It's not the Amsterdam that tourists tend to idolize, but its homes still mimic the scale of the canal row houses built between the fifteenth and nineteenth centuries inside the historic core's concentric rings of canals encircled by the singelgracht, or beltway canal. This context is important because the Ijburg district has become a place of architectural experimentation set apart from the old city, similar to the Ørestad neighborhood outside Copenhagen or Porte de Clichy and Seine-Saint-Denis in northwestern Paris, skirting the Boulevard Périphérique.

The other important context has to do with the color of Houten Herenhuis' façade. Standing just a few stories tall, the edifice is in line with other canal homes of its ilk, per local codes, and its deep-red hue is a nod to the bricks densely formed from river clay that define old Amsterdam. (Even the word "brick" derives, in part, from the Old Dutch brike or bricke.) Technically, however, the façade is Swedish red, or Falun red, named for the copper-mining byproduct unearthed near the Swedish city of Falun for hundreds of years and used on barns in Scandinavia, yet it appears recognizably urban for denizens of the Low Countries.

Inside, a far more neutral palette is achieved with unfinished spruce CLT panels, whose grain offers a ribbon effect that unites different rooms despite the programmatic shifts that each level of the home represents. It also unites the living spaces with the all-important staircase, which is both circulation and a room unto itself pushed to one side (leaving the floor plan reasonably open). As capacious as the interior feels, the panels offer natural acoustic dampening and warmth and make it feel more intimate, which drove the clients' original motives and inadvertently transformed the architect's scope of work in the years that followed. On the strength of its application at Houten Herenhuis, Lenders also clad her own offices with different spruce CLT panels to achieve the same warmth, as well as to monitor how it ages so they can inform future clients of the product's performance capabilities.

Inside, a far more neutral palette is achieved with unfinished spruce CLT panels, whose grain offers a ribbon effect that unites different rooms despite the programmatic shifts that each level of the home represents.

"In the Netherlands there are few forests, and therefore there is little wood production and no CLT factory. For our construction projects, we mainly use CLT from Germany, which is made from spruce," says Lenders. "In my office, I placed walls with different sight qualities, to show the clients what to expect. In a project that has to be affordable, we usually use the industrial grade, which the client should know has more knots in it and, sometimes, stains or small holes. Also, you may see resin leaking from the panel in the beginning. After all, it's a natural product."

She says her clients also report occasional loud bangs because the wood, itself, is expanding and contracting and sometimes splitting—a common refrain heard by architects around the world who use CLT panels in their residential work. And like all architects who work with CLT panels, Lenders isn't perturbed in the least.

"Wood, as a natural material, has its own story because it has lived. Surrounded by this organic material, people feel connected to the natural environment."

The bones of the building consist of glue-laminated timber and cross-laminated spruce panels, forming the super-structure on the relatively soft, reclaimed land of Ijburg. However, when Lenders started working on it in 2007, there was virtually no infrastructure or pipeline for solid wood in the Netherlands. So, she approached contractor Kerkhofs Houtbouw, who had recently completed a spruce CLT pavilion atop a Rotterdam roof. Through Kerkhofs, Lenders got in touch with a German draftsman and installer and drew up the 3-D production model of the timber construction herself. That was a swift learning experience in practice, and a convincing encounter with timber construction prefabrication. During assembly, everything fit perfectly.

But Lenders suspected that the modest spans required by a narrow Dutch canal home might work perfectly with mass timber, and to achieve it she complied with the Dutch "Bouwbesluit," which provides rules on structural safety, fire safety, and acoustics. This also applied to wood.

A 2019 Dutch television special on timber construction is sometimes cited by architects in the Netherlands as a watershed moment when mass timber went from fringe pursuit to sanctioned strategy. Two years later, Amsterdam mandated that at least 20 percent of all new residential construction must be timber by 2025—on the heels of other mandates across Europe, including the 2020 decree in France that all new public buildings must be at least 50 percent timber or other natural materials by 2022. The political will in European countries to explore timber as a quick-to-install and easy-to-specify renewable material, in other words, was finally catching up with what Lenders knew all along.

"We are happy to design all our projects with wood and bio-based materials," says Lenders, "and I hope that our projects will inspire others, sparking a collective passion to shape a healthier, more sustainable world together."

1 Entrance
2 Storage
3 Studio
4 Bedroom
5 Bedroom
6 Kitchen
7 Dining
8 Living
9 Rooftop Terrace
10 Balcony

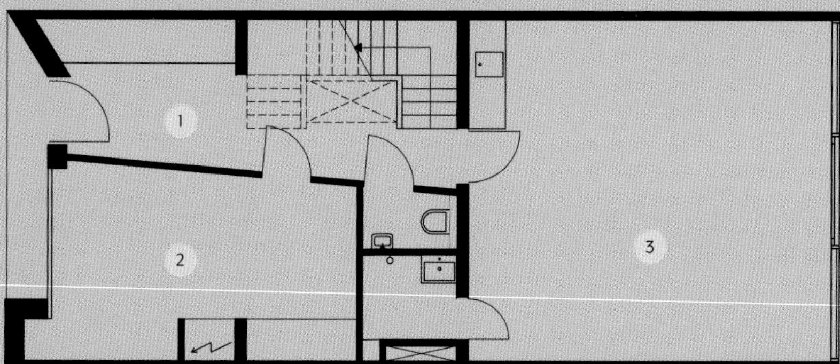

GROUND FLOOR

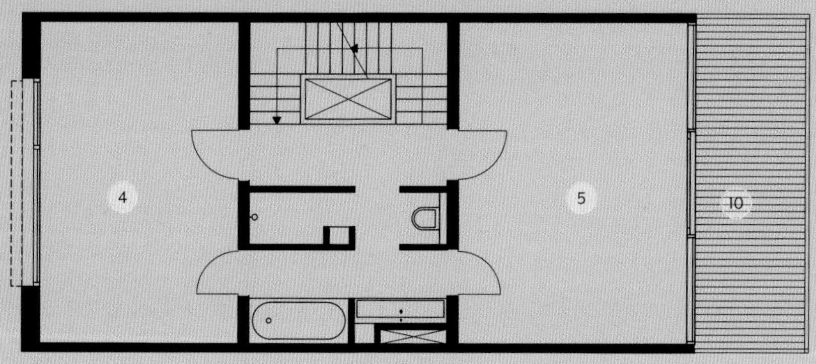

FIRST FLOOR

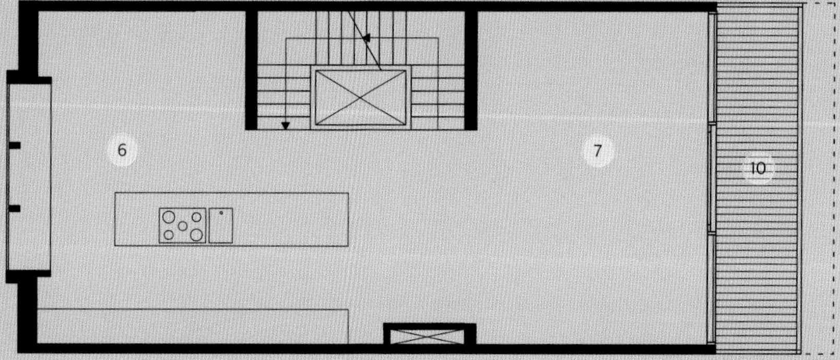

SECOND FLOOR

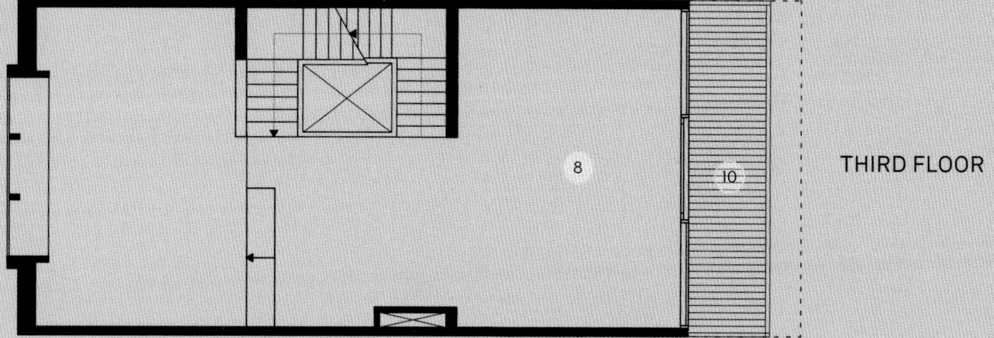

THIRD FLOOR

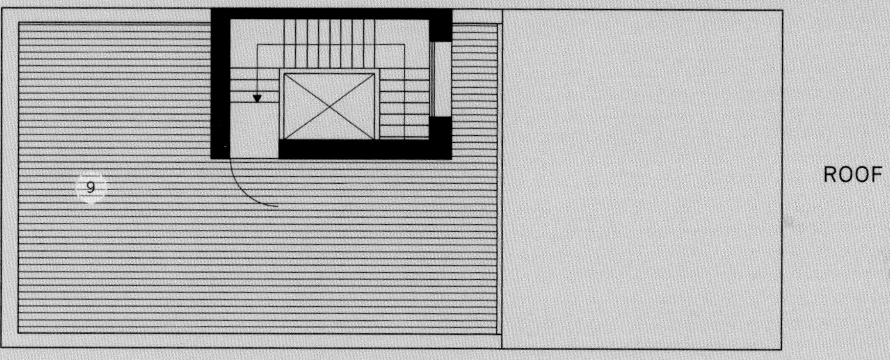

ROOF

0   10 m

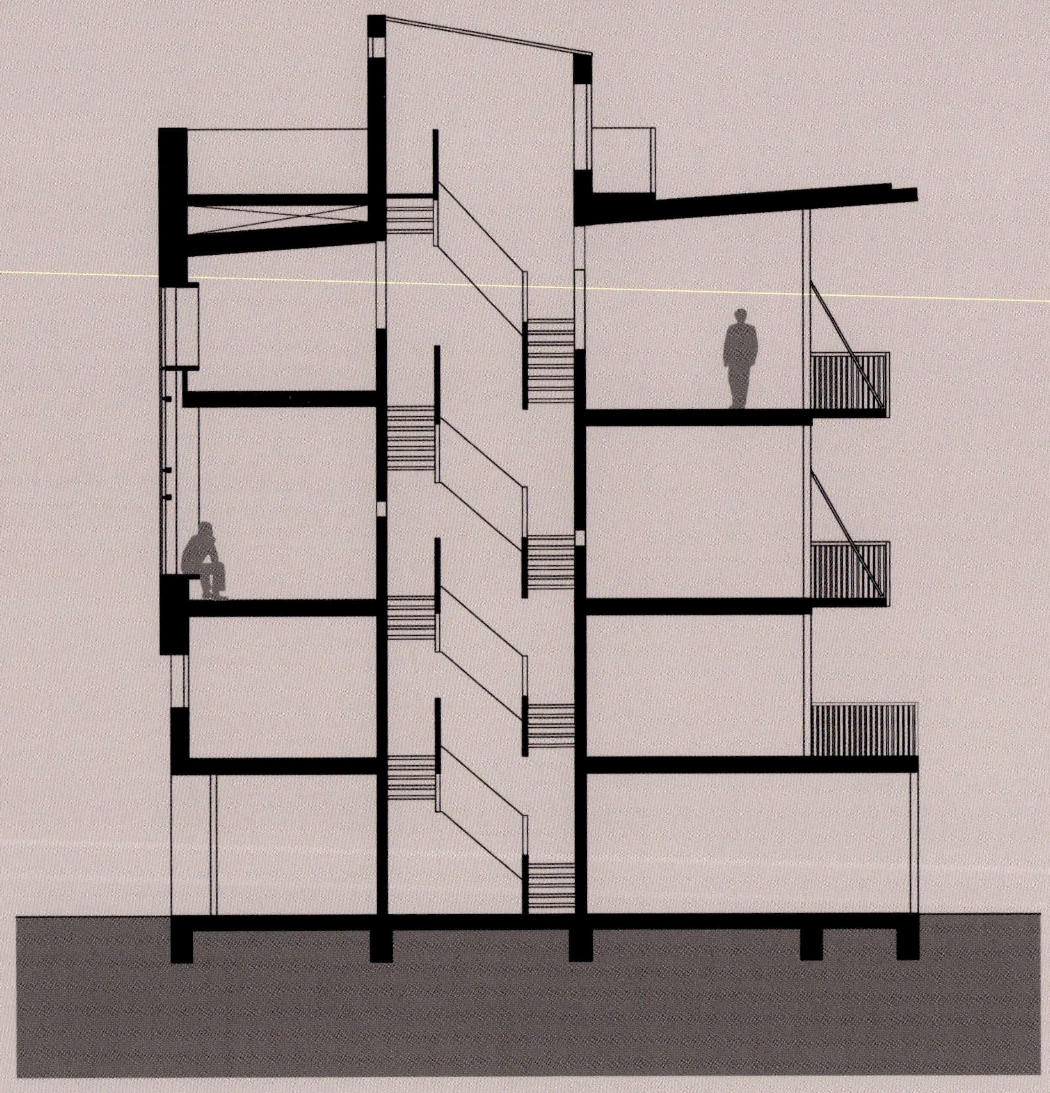

LONGITUDINAL SECTION

0   10 m

CROSS SECTION

GUDBRANDSLIE CABIN

Filefjell, Norway
Helen & Hard
2015

In 2015, the Norwegian architecture firm Helen & Hard completed Gudbrandslie Cabin near Tyinkrysset, Filefjell, at the center of southern Norway, adjacent to Jotunheimen National Park. It's a rural area, equidistant to Oslo and Bergen, where it snows most days of the week and winds can pick up to 20 miles per hour, which is slightly more than a breeze and enough to feel the bite. As a shelter, it would be easy to conceive a structure in this sort of place to act as a formidable barrier against nature, creating wind sheers on the ground nearby and all but ensuring that a snowbank develops to one side. Gudbrandslie Cabin, on the other hand, is just the opposite—a sympathetic form that works with the wind and snow and shelters a small family and two Oslo lawyers during weekend retreats.

"The wind in Norway—especially high in the mountains—is so challenging and so important to think about. You need to create places where you can be protected and sit in the sun to warm up, but you also need to accommodate the wind's movement," says the project's architect, Reinhard Kropf, "and that's where the snow comes in too—and it's a fact of life that when you arrive at your cabin for the weekend, you have to spend an hour digging it out."

"What we are trying to do at Helen & Hard is bring back the timber tradition, using today's digital technology and know-how about material," says the project's architect, Reinhard Kropf. "In this case, with the cabin, we wanted to limit the joints and connections—because that's what we needed to do here."

To make such a modest impact on the landscape, Kropf developed a series of wind studies for the site, using a Rhino software plug-in, ultimately shaping the roof in line with the land and creating an L-shaped home, which opens toward a view (as you would expect) and backs in to the hillside as it slopes southwest. The property is the highest point on the hill, above the line of other nearby cabins, most of which is rather muddy owing to the saturated ground. The best ground for the concrete foundations, according to Kropf, is along the north of the property, where the L shape can also conceal the living areas from the access road that bisects the site.

Wind studies. Snowbanks. Mandatory snow shoveling. Mud. It all sounds rather unromantic, but logistics are everything to this project, whose remoteness was an important factor in Kropf's choice of prefabricated, cross-laminated timber panels to sit on the concrete plinth, trucked in and clad on-site.

"It's costly to build on such a site—and it was an advantage to have a higher degree of prefabrication and finish, which meant less assembly time," says Kropf. "What we learned from this project is that you can manage complex geometries with CLT. It's not that much more expensive, either, because you can be precise in the prefabrication process— there's less waste."

Kropf's complex geometries, generated and translated from the wind studies, are what largely define the architecture's appearance from the outside. In plan, the cabin is a polygon, with no fewer than seven faces, and in section the two-story structure has no fewer than five level changes. But it's in elevation where the mass timber project seems to really defy expectations. The CLT panels don't articulate forms by using the strict laws of modular building, as they do in many mass timber buildings (particularly low- and high-rise structures), so much as they sculpt spaces by using the elemental forces of geostrophic wind. The house appears to cosset the hillside, and the CLT panels, in turn, appear to cosset the interior volumes, where built-in furniture appears to hug the walls, stairs appear to ripple into pools, and fluid spaces signal programmatic shifts with a subtle cant of the wall and ceiling. There's a sense of seamlessness throughout the spaces even in spite of the level changes and contouring of the cabin's interior and exterior surfaces. It is, you could almost say, the same way that human skin hugs muscles and bones.

Kropf's complex geometries, generated and translated from the wind studies, are what largely define the architecture's appearance from the outside and in parts of the interior.

That's not an accident. Kropf calls it a "skeleton and cladding" strategy, which he says is a way of recovering the timber traditions of Scandinavia before the oil revolution.

"What we are trying to do at Helen & Hard is bring back the timber tradition by using today's digital technology and know-how about material," he says. "In this case, with the cabin, we wanted to limit the joints and connections—because that's what we needed to do here. We asked about the local possibilities and the client's needs, and we had to create a hybrid approach that worked with the site."

This notion of architecture representing a site's or a program's logic rather than an architect's logic, so to speak, is something that you find in Helen & Hard's other projects. Their atrium in their 2019 Financial Park project in Oslo (with SAAHA Architects) might seem like an Escherian fantasy, but ramps offer direct connections for people rather than forcing them to heed symmetry and walk all the way around a big empty space just to reach the other side. Their 2020 community building called Samling for the remote town of Sand, Norway, might combine a bank, library, office, and ten residences, but they ignored all of the historical, abstract geometries of what a "bank" or a "library" or an "office" should look like. Instead, they asked how the functions they represent could be available to the community and its residents, who would rely on this building for much more than just banking, reading, or working.

"The wind in Norway—especially high in the mountains—is so challenging and so important to think about. You need to create places where you can be protected and sit in the sun to warm up, but you also need to accommodate the wind's movement," says the project's architect, Reinhard Kropf.

Helen & Hard's Nordic Pavilion for the 2021 Venice Biennale, titled "What We Share," epitomizes their approach to privileging purpose as a driver of form. The pavilion was constructed of milled-spruce stanchions, seating, shelves, and stairs that offered a variety of private and semiprivate spaces that featured text and video. It was not an experience focused on pushing information or a point of view, necessarily, as many Biennale pavilions do, but rather a focused opportunity for visitors to appreciate being among others. Even at the pandemic's peak, "what we share" was durable enough as a theme to withstand snark or even despair, because it wasn't, as Helen & Hard saw it, an interrogative, but rather an imperative—a paean to communal living in principle and cohousing in particular that raised the issue of ownership and privacy. What do we really own in this world that cannot be taken or bought? Is it reasonable to expect privacy in any other circumstance beyond solitude? Why do we design and build anything, in the first place—to resist the force of community?

The answer, of course, is to see community as a force that's as elemental as wind. And in the case of Gudbrandslie Cabin, as with all of Helen & Hard's work, there is no point in resisting what comes naturally to all of us.

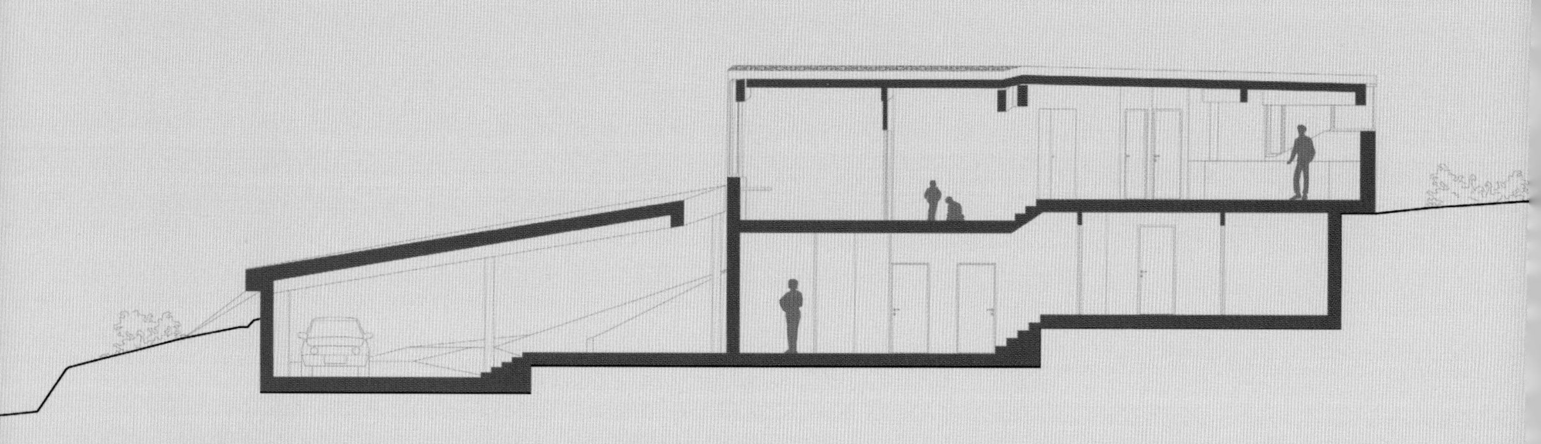

THE RYE

London, England
Tikari Works
2020

Peckham is an area of greater London that is not gentrified or even necessarily gentrifying (although the proposed redevelopment of its local covered market, called Aylesham Centre, is at risk these days). It exists as a multicultural enclave that's just four stops from London Bridge on the Overground train, but a world apart from selfie-snapping tourists at Francis Drake's Golden Hinde or the Yeoman Warders' Tower. Here Afro-Caribbean, Chinese, Indian, and Turkish bars, beauty shops, and markets line its main artery, Rye Lane, which extends north and south, skirting the area's namesake treasure, a 50-acre park where William Blake reportedly had a vision of angels in an oak tree. As early as the 1840s, frontage on the park became desirable for leaseholders and freeholders alike, and today there are single-family Victorian and Edwardian homes along the four streets that encircle Peckham Rye Common, as well as brick-clad postwar apartment complexes.

The husband-and-wife team at Tikari Works, Ty and Nicola, have designed and developed the Rye in Peckham Rye, London, a two-building, ten-unit residential project constructed with cross-laminated timber panels.

It's here that the husband-and-wife team at Tikari Works, Ty and Nicola, have designed and developed the Rye, a two-building, ten-unit residential project constructed with cross-laminated timber panels. It's a singular contribution to Peckham Rye, which is a patchwork of private developments that have shaped this area of south London over the last 150 years to be a comfortable and relatively quiet bedroom community for commuters and families. For that reason, the broader area around Sydenham Hill ridge has presented unique opportunities for architects, contractors, and their clients to approach renovation and infill under almost the opposite circumstances of London north of the Thames River, whose real estate prices have jumped by double digits in the postpandemic years.

Tikari Works, which does most of its work south of the Thames, routinely takes on all three roles of architect, contractor, and client and has developed several properties—including the Rye—that share a single agenda focused on environmental impact, buildability, and architectural intent. It's what cofounder Ty Tikari calls a Venn diagram for the firm that also serves as an ethical foundation for its work.

"We're looking at how design decisions can inform the drivers of these three aspects of our practice, and CLT fits neatly into the diagram right in the middle," he says, "because CLT, as a design driver, is inherently an efficient strategy for building. Mass timber is a total solution if you're the architect, client, and builder."

Ty Tikari points to the biophilic aspects of CLT
that make the interiors of the Rye an ideal
counterpoint to its urban context.

Tikari, wearing his owner and builder hats, points to the precision that off-site manufactured panels afford, as well as the swiftness of their delivery and assembly as core aspects of CLT's total solution. It's about an economy of scale that works when CLT is used on a multiunit development. "The initial outlay [for CLT] was slightly more than a traditional concrete frame would be, but the savings you're getting on bank interest and follow-on trades and minimizing waste and construction time—it adds up to be a benefit," he says.

Wearing his architect hat, on the other hand, Tikari points to the biophilic aspects of CLT that make the interiors an ideal counterpoint to an urban context—the acoustic absorption and attenuation softens the spaces, as does the warmth of natural wood's look and feel. Here, as with most CLT projects built over the last ten years, you will still find areas where the spruce panels express sap in small beads and rivulets. You have to really hunt for it upon entering any of the rooms, but once you see the walls weeping ever so slightly, it's impossible not to notice. And here, as with most CLT projects, you will also find areas near the windows that the sun has faded, in contrast to the areas farthest from the windows, which still bear the original, honeyed hues of the unfinished spruce.

The 9,400-square-foot site that Tikari Works purchased as freeholder and developer has one frontage along Peckham Rye—the high street along the park—and one along Kinsale Road, which pulls a dogleg curve to wrap around the southern and western edges of the property. Facing the park, the Rye's larger building rises three levels before steeply backing off the frontal plane (breaking at the precise height of the eave line of the next-door building) and flattening out. Facing the western edge of the site along Kinsale Road, the Rye's smaller building keeps a gable roof form and blends in with the more modestly scaled row houses there. Cladding the entire project from top to bottom, front to back, are 10,000 mottled clay shingles that were handmade at the Petersen Tegl factory in Denmark. In an even, gray light, they're chestnut and russet brown, but in the sun the shingles can even appear copper or tawny in spots, and the variation draws in the hues and moods of the Victorian- and Edwardian-era homes, especially, on the surrounding blocks. That might seem like a pithy observation, but it's impossible to overstate the intensity of brown brick in this area, whose only relief is white trim or a brightly colored door.

"The forms [of the Rye] were clearly outside of what you'd expect of a housing development there, so the tiles help them, because we didn't want to go so far beyond the line—and create something threatening for the neighborhood. That's where materiality came in," says Tikari, "to bring the forms back into a realm that's more comforting. London is a brick city. The shingles by Petersen are similar to brick in terms of how they're made and how they look, so we were able to realize the tension without it being eerie for people."

"The forms [of the Rye] were clearly outside of what you'd expect of a housing development there, so the tiles help them, because we didn't want to go so far beyond the line—and create something threatening for the neighborhood. That's where materiality came in," says Tikari.

In between the two structures is a sunken green space that includes courtyards for the ground-floor units that are built within the concrete plinths of the main structures (cleverly united in the middle by a perforated parapet). It's hard to believe there are ten different units at the Rye, since both buildings read as single-family homes. But the overall project reveals itself slowly on a walk around the block to be a clever and economical use of space while also offering generous allotments for tenants. In doing so, Tikari Works participates in the broader economic experiment of community building in this neighborhood by doing two things well: adding to the housing stock and maintaining a high architectural standard. But the firm also advances that broader experiment by doing two things *incredibly* well: enriching the neighborhood's context and employing a renewable material whose embodied carbon footprint is a fraction of what it might have been in conventional development. Paring the Rye back to what it wanted to be, as an expression of CLT panels, delivered something that London needed it to be: a sustainable solution for cheerful homes to build housing stock and a capital investment for an entrepreneurial architecture firm to prosper.

PECKHAM RYE
KINSALE ROAD
EAST DULWICH ROAD
10m
50m

KINSALE BLOCK

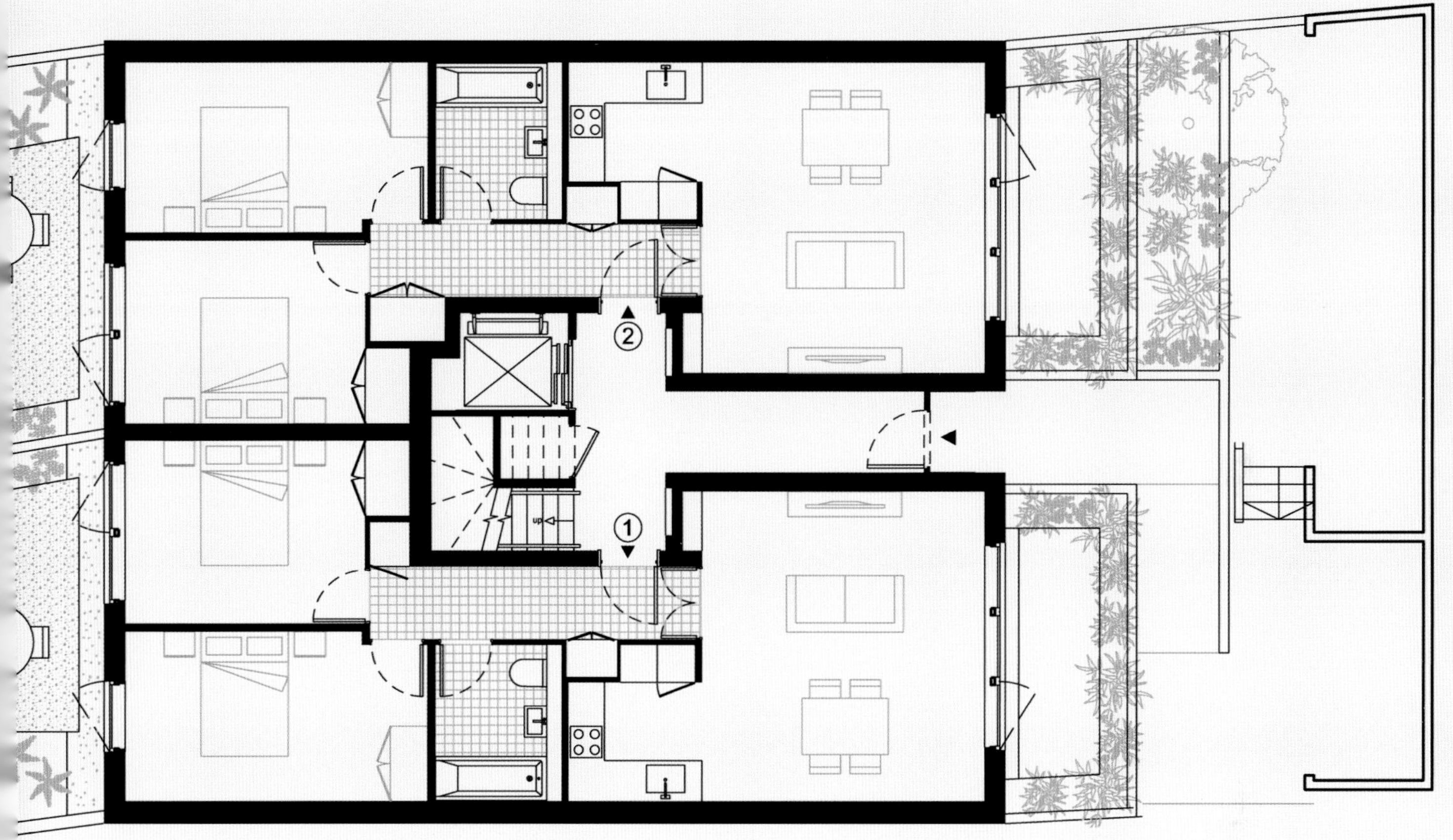

PARK BLOCK

R11 LOFT EXTENSION

Munich, Germany
Pool Leber Architekten
2018

Among mass timber's virtues for residential architecture, its lightness is often overlooked in favor of its impressively short build times, its potential to contribute to the decarbonization of the construction industry, and the biophilic qualities of wood as a material. But its lightness is precisely what makes the R11 Loft Extension, by the Munich firm Pool Leber Architekten, important for this site and similar urban sites across Europe.

Pool Leber founders and design principals Isabella Leber and Martin Pool completed the loft atop a 1987 building in the Maxvorstadt neighborhood of central Munich on one of the city's oldest streets. Despite the building's relatively young age, the foundations of the existing block would not have handled the weight of a conventionally built addition consisting entirely of reinforced concrete, so Leber and Pool opted for a hybrid structure of CLT panels clad in steel to enclose not one but two new floors, as well as a mezzanine (with only the lateral side walls completed in concrete).

On one of Munich's oldest streets, Pool Leber founders Isabella Leber and Martin Pool completed the loft atop a 1987 building in the Maxvorstadt neighborhood.

"Right from the start we knew what to do because we'd [already] done a two-floor addition to a building in Munich, and we had the same problem there with a weak foundation—so we knew we had to use CLT again," says Isabella Leber. "Concrete and glass are cultural for us in Europe, in that they are typical materials for massive projects like housing, but timber is also cultural—maybe not in a postwar context, but certainly in a prewar one."

While the outside of the building might seem acontextual by the standards of Munich's architectural history, it is entirely contextual when you consider the pre- and postwar crucible of Munich's urban development. Nearly all the buildings in its central Altstadt historic district (adjacent to Maxvorstadt) were destroyed by Allied bombers during World War II, which is a little hard to believe if you were to see it today, since the city has been faithfully rebuilt to match what was razed. It's not exactly an ersatz rendition of Munich, ca. 1939, as much as it is a reproduction—meaning you have to squint only a little in its central Marienplatz to think you're seeing the real McCoy. Similarly, the site occupied by R11's building is also surrounded by postwar reconstructions, as well as examples of ex novo infill from the late 20th century—including some examples of high-style postmodernism, which are easy to spot—making "context" in Maxvorstadt seem a little less like prewar Munich and little more like postwar Rotterdam.

Atop a four-story building, it shouldn't surprise anyone that Pool Leber's clients wanted decent views of the surrounding area from its south-facing façade and a generously sized balcony. It was to be as much of a home as it was to be an entertaining space, where they could enjoy the balcony culture that Leber says is critical to the health of all German cities, not just the Bavarian capital city. "The opportunity to be outside is important," says Leber, "and our clients left a lot up to us to determine the spaces inside."

Across 10,225 gross square feet, half inside and half outside, the architects created flexibility for the clients. "The opportunity to be outside is important," says Leber.

One room weaves into the next across 10,225 gross square feet of space (about half of which is interior livable space that includes three bedrooms), all of which fulfills the brief for a fluid indoor-outdoor lifestyle, particularly in the summertime. The walls are gently angled, even when they are cut in unusual ways—all the product of several key studies undertaken by the design team to evaluate how light would be distributed and reach as deeply as possible into the spaces with only one major southern exposure. (The design team included Pool and Leber, as well as Valeria Polakovicova, Johannes Sailer, and Joanna Tomaszewska.)

Pool and Leber also had to evaluate how to distribute the weight of the new three-story structure, considering the weak foundation of the building. Yet, as luminous as the space is and as light as they had to make their intervention, the design team created a sense of elemental heft. The concrete firewalls on either side are left untreated and unsmoothed, revealing the thin lines of the formwork. The spaces alternate between low ceilings and vaulted ceilings, all in spruce CLT panels from Austria, which, at times, make the home feel like a wooden cathedral.

Concrete firewalls on either side of the interior volume are left untreated and unsmoothed, revealing the thin lines of the formwork.

Leber says her firm will continue to work with CLT, especially having found a local builder who specializes in installing them for the R11 loft project, which took—start to finish—three days to complete. It's a decision that's as much environmental as it is practical for the kind of work they do on tight urban sites.

"For us, mass timber construction is one of a lot of options. But I think the benefit of mass timber is reachable only if you use it to meet specific requirements," she says. "For that reason, mass timber might not be feasible always, but it can be really good for interventions—for smaller-scale projects that might fit into or on top of existing structures. We are very close to Austria in southern Germany—and so it's not a matter of being close to the source. It's a matter of, culturally, what is possible."

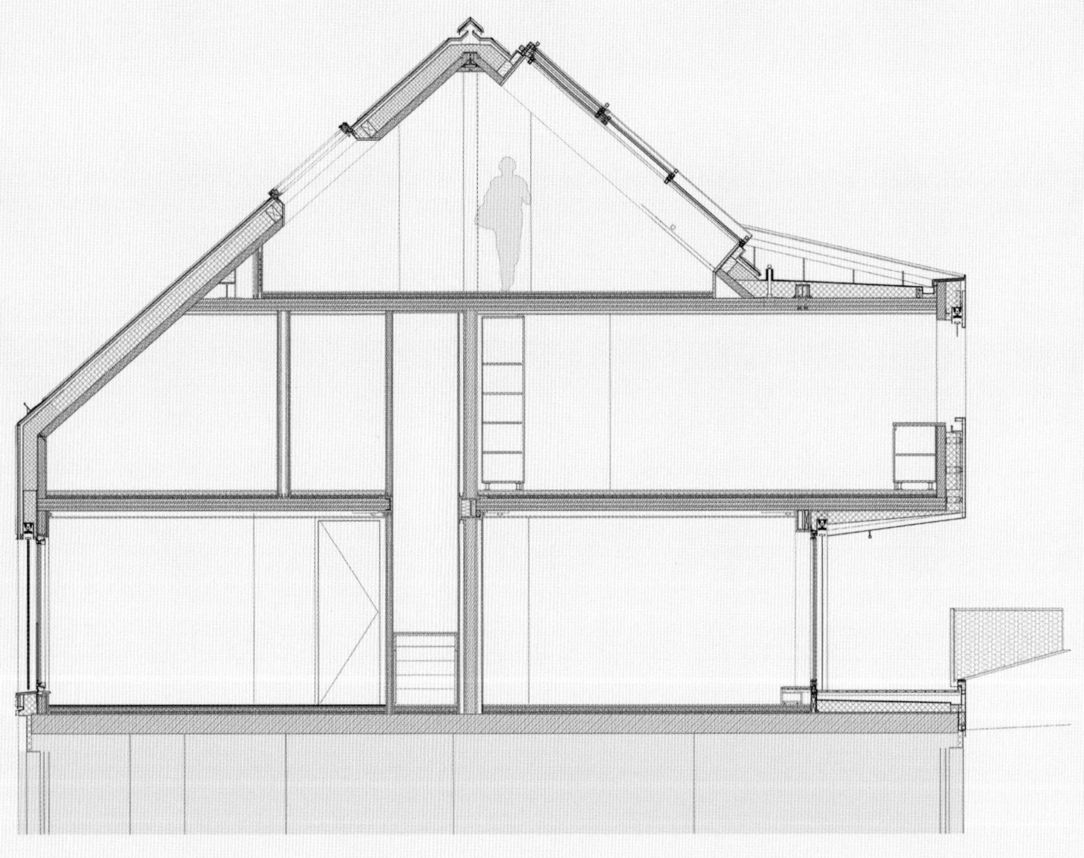

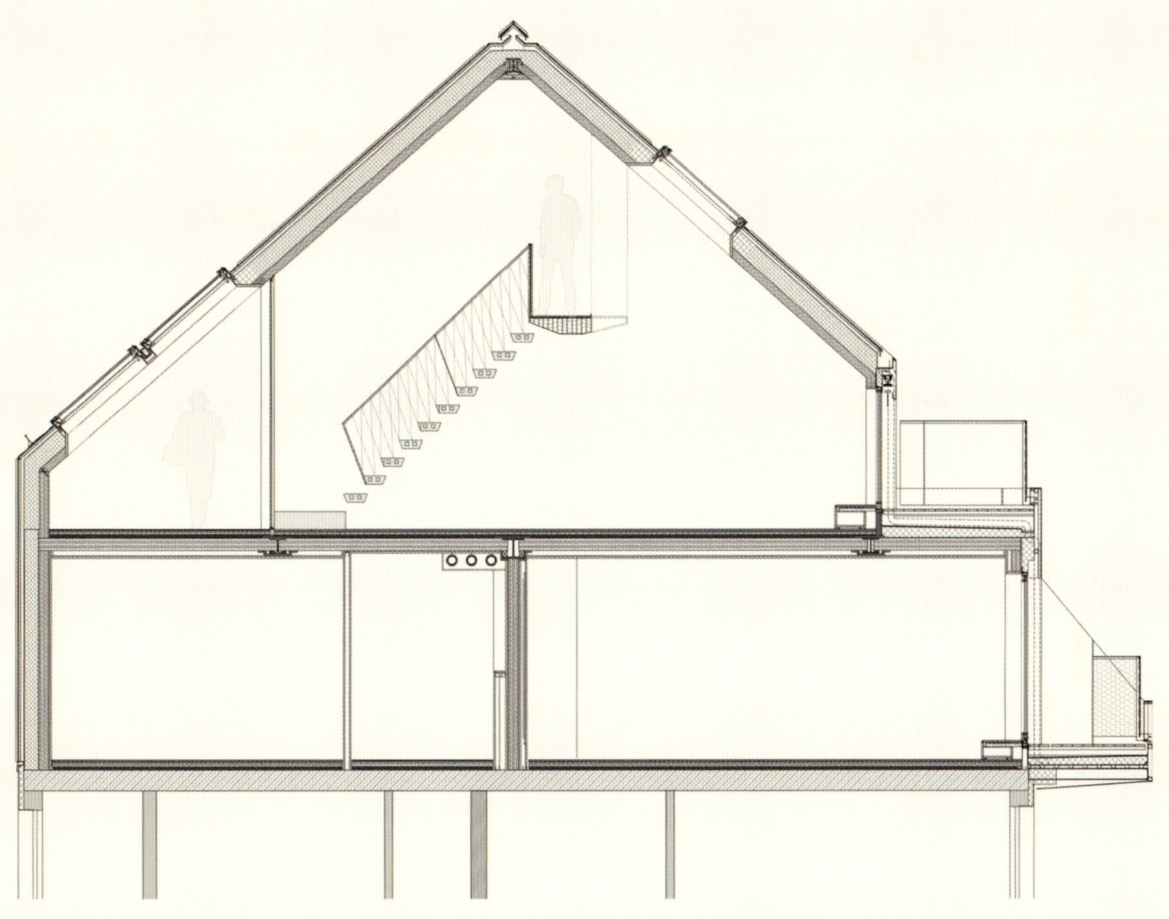

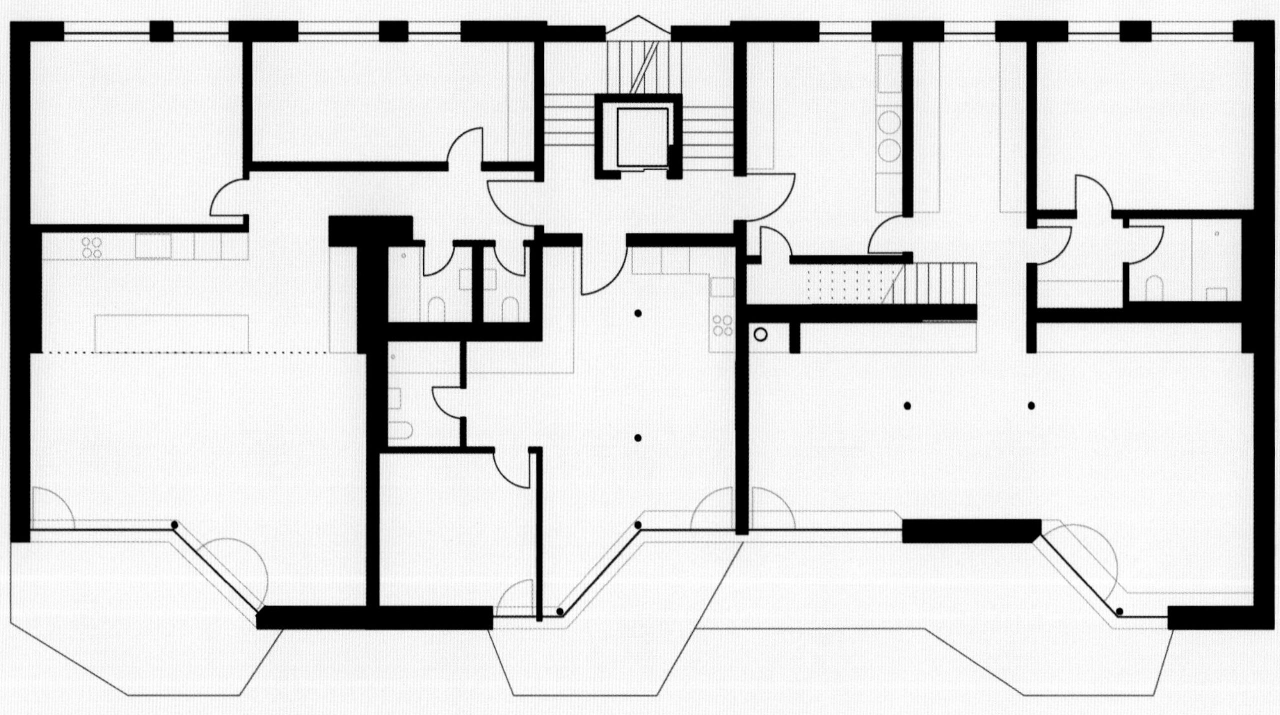

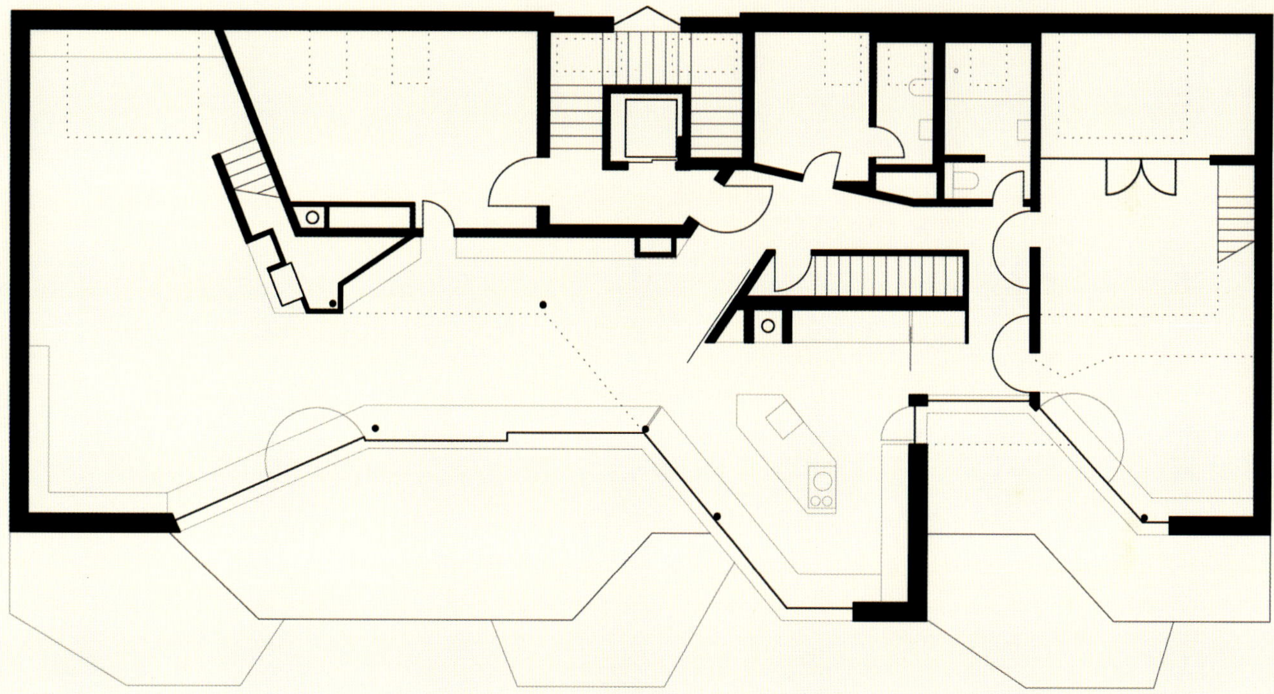

BROOKLYN MASS TIMBER HOUSE

Brooklyn, New York, USA
Schiller Projects
2023

Schiller Projects' renovation of a 150-year-old Brooklyn carriage house using mass timber is a master class in adapting a contributing structure while also pivoting toward a hopeful future. There's still garage space for a car—a prize for any homeowner in New York's five boroughs—but there is scant evidence inside the envelope that this was ever a place for carriages, Model Ts, Studebakers, or limousines in its most recent chapter. Aaron Schiller, founder and principal of his eponymous firm, is both the designer and the owner of this home, which he created for his growing family (now totaling four). He transformed the carriage house's two levels and added a third along a narrow site to create 4,000 square feet of indoor and outdoor living and entertaining spaces.

You can find lots of carriage houses in the alleys of Boston, Baltimore, and Washington, DC, but this one, handsomely renovated by Schiller Projects, fronts a main road named for Cornelius Vanderbilt, no less, that knits together the Fort Greene and Clinton Hill neighborhoods of Brooklyn.

The ground-floor cooking, dining, and entertaining
space formerly housed limousines and, long
before that, the carriages of nineteenth-century
Brooklyn. The backyard, still incomplete in this
photograph, is the lure no matter the weather.

A unified kitchen and dining area on the ground floor opens onto a generous backyard, the living space on the second floor overlooks the main street, and two bedrooms toward the back overlook the backyard—forming the family's principal private space. A primary suite on the newly created third floor opens to a roof terrace overlooking Our Queen of All Saints Brooklyn, completed in 1878 and designed by Gustave Steinbeck—one of three consecrated cathedrals in the city along with St. John the Divine and St. Patrick's in Manhattan. All Saints is a Gothic jewel box reportedly inspired by the two-level Sainte-Chapelle de Paris on the Île de la Cité, completed in 1248, but perhaps more accurately modeled on the Sainte-Chapelle de Vincennes outside Paris, completed in 1552, whose sanctuary is one large space, not two levels. Quibbles aside, it's the view that matters, and from that third-floor perch above the carriage house, all the eye can see are Steinbeck's delicate trefoil windows along the nave.

"It's my favorite thing about the neighborhood," says Schiller, "and instead of pivoting the house toward the backyard, as a lot of row-house renovations do in the city, we pivoted everything to the front—the living area where the kids play and the bedroom where you wake up in the morning."

Schiller bought the property with the express purpose of marrying adaptive reuse to timber, in a gambit to minimize carbon and the physical waste that all construction kicks up. For this project, though, timber's lightness for the third-floor pop-up and interior interventions was perfectly aligned with the requirements of a ca. 1870s garage whose foundation was as fragile as any building from the era. Schiller, who has since sold the property, says that even if he was working in a historic district, he found some welcomed flexibility with its authorities, who allowed him to use larger triple-glazed windows than the building would have had originally—adapting what he calls the rubric for success.

You can still find lots of intact carriage houses in neighborhoods such as Capitol Hill in Washington, DC, and Beacon Hill in Boston, usually off an alley and likely transformed into residences within the last thirty years. Walking along the sidewalk, you might have once been able to trace an arc of road apples and motor oil from the street right up to their massive doors. In recent decades, that evidence of their purpose has been replaced by welcome mats and planters—making their frontages cottage-like and making their discovery in a back alley quaint.

The Schillers' carriage house, on the other hand, fronts a main road named for Cornelius Vanderbilt that knits together the Fort Greene and Clinton Hill neighborhoods. The vintage of this carriage house maps to one important chapter in Brooklyn's growth, largely spurred by local merchant-millionaires and industry's magnates, whose speculative residential developments participated in the day's architectural styles with Queen Anne turrets, Gothic Revival spires, and the Italianate eaves. The 1870s were the early years of the "brown decades," in the words of Lewis Mumford, prior to the go-go of the Gilded Age in fin-de-siècle America—a twenty-five-year period when northern American cities were made and remade both by industry's wealth and the largest waves of immigration the country had seen to date. Long before it was connected to Manhattan via subway, Brooklyn experienced exponential growth in these years, and it needed new roads. You can see in maps of Fort Greene and Clinton Hill pockets of gridded streets uniformly filling the gaps decade by decade between established avenues (many shadowing native footpaths) that usually stemmed inland from the docks of the East River.

Vanderbilt Avenue was created as a thoroughfare from the Brooklyn Navy Yard in the north to Grand Army Plaza to the south. It would have been among the first streets in Brooklyn to be electrified. It would have been among the busiest right away, connecting the commercial corridor of Atlantic Avenue with area residents. Any project there (in any era) would have been a plum commission for any architect. What this era demanded, for Schiller, was something more than a handsome renovation.

"There is the context of Clinton Hill and the context of the architectural ambition here—both quite different. Timber makes you think regionally and globally. Clinton Hill made me think more locally as a contributor to the neighborhood," says Schiller.

Thinking locally took him to New England, at first, though, to source his glulam beams. Looking to achieve the elusive economics of scale, Schiller scoured the East Coast of the US for institutional mass timber projects with a much-larger shipment of material he could piggyback onto. He finally found a 350,000-square-foot dormitory whose supplier, Kalesnikoff, was willing to work with him on his own 4,000-square-foot project. He asked Kalesnikoff to supply the same material as the dorm for the same price and delivered it to the same jobsite—and he rented a truck to fetch his Douglas fir glulam beams and plates.

"In the Nordic countries, I see mass timber all the time. Not here, though, so it's a resource issue," he says. "If I do a building in steel, there are five hundred people who can sell me an I beam right now, and it arrives in three days. Glulam might, on the other hand, be out of stock for six months because the factory in Tennessee is running behind. So, there are supply challenges, and, for that reason, you don't design a timber building and then go, "This is how it looks, and let's make it." You work the other way around. You figure out how to make the building first and then decide what it'll look like."

Arguably the star of the project is the staircase circumnavigating a small atrium that connects the three levels of the home. Graced by a tiny Japanese maple and a place apart from the rest of the house, this vertical zone's slatted treads grip the foot, some of which shoot up as balusters to create the bones of the atrium's volume. New Hampshire—based builder Bensonwood fabricated the glulam panels, which Schiller reports came on the heels of months of conversations about how to retrofit this carriage house to be a real home.

"The stairs had something like 8,200 different connections, and we had discussion down to the individual screw. So, what you see is really the product of a building as design, and it really influenced my firm to think differently," he says. "The making of it—whatever we're doing—is how we think about things today, thanks, in part, to those stairs."

Schiller worked with Stickbulb to create
"electrified laminated timber" (ELT), which
carries LED strips at the chamfered breaks in
the panels every 4 feet.

The other star of the show is the lighting, which Schiller worked on with Long Island City manufacturer Stickbulb to create what he calls "electrified laminated timber," or ELT, and for which he has a patent pending. The chamfered breaks in every ceiling panel reveal small channels that can carry LED lighting, which offer an elegant alternative to the overhead fixture and, since they're embedded equally across the ceiling, carry the eye across the rooms at 4-foot intervals. Integrated and syncopated lines create rhythm and reduce the amount of energy required to light the place from front to back (although the atrium does a fine job of illuminating the middle of the structure, even on gray days, without any artificial light at all).

Would Schiller do it again? Undoubtedly, he says. The weight of working with solid, large-scale material such as glulam forced him to think about the space as a series of "big moves," and not a series of smaller design moves.

"Designing for solid masses of material is different from designing for little sticks that you're trying to assemble. It's more satisfying," says Schiller. "There's a sense of weight to working with a solid, large-scale material, and there's a solidity to the building that influences you."

CELLAR
1 Planter
2 Cellar

FIRST FLOOR
1 Garage
2 Kitchen
3 Dining
4 Ground-Floor Bathroom
5 Backyard

SECOND FLOOR
1 Living Room
2 Laundry
3 Full Bathroom 1
4 Full Bathroom 2
5 Bedroom 1
6 Bedroom 2

THIRD FLOOR
1 Roof Terrace
2 Primary Bedroom
3 Primary Bathroom
4 Closet

CELLAR   FIRST FLOOR

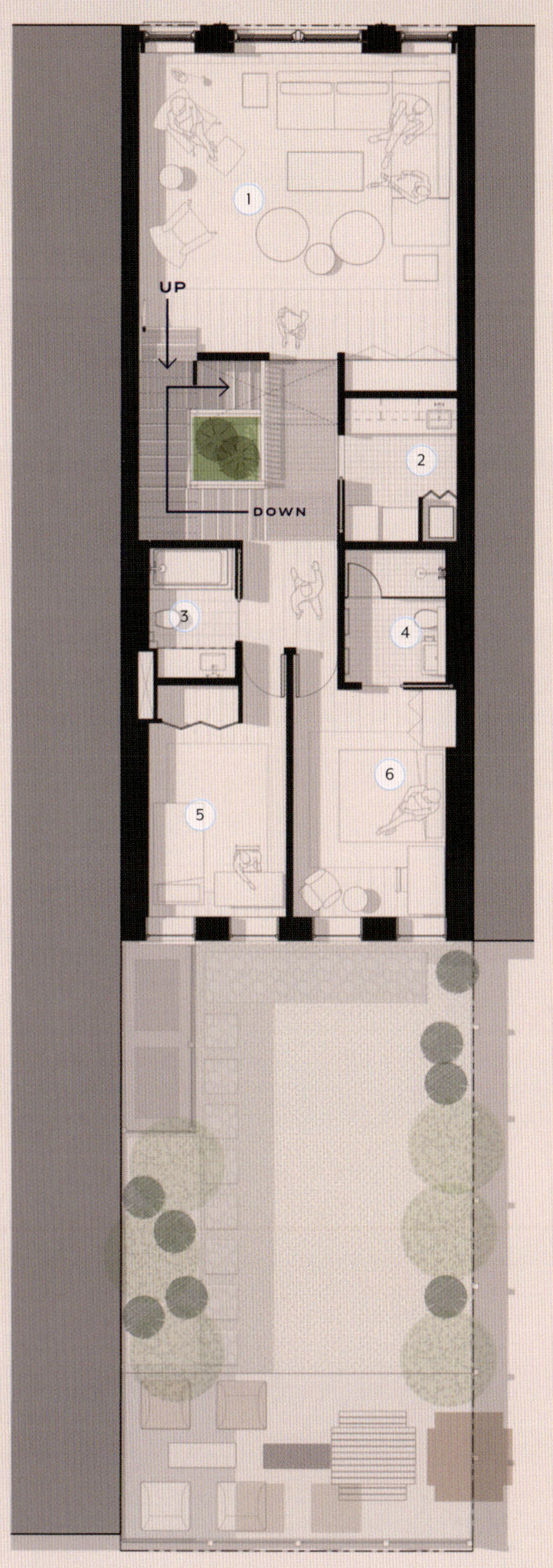

SECOND FLOOR

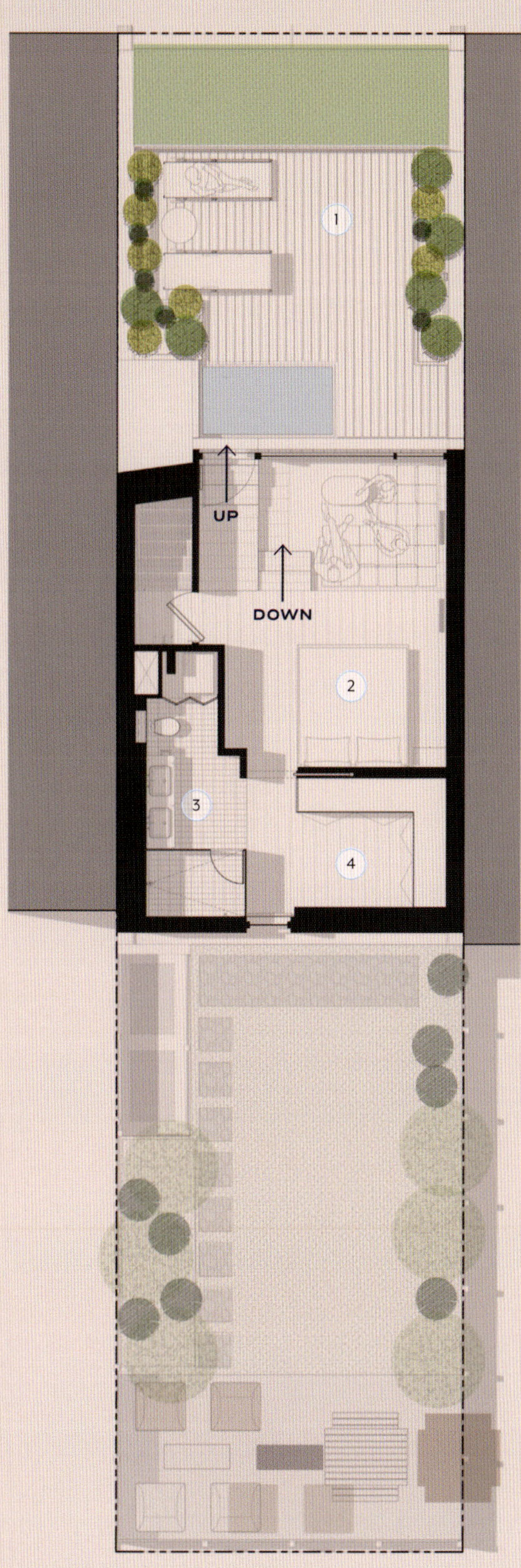

THIRD-FLOOR ADDITION

CREDITS

HAUS GABLES
Project Team: Jennifer Bonner, Ben Halpern, Benzi Rodman, Justin Jiang, Dohyun Lee, Daniela Leon
CLT Manufacturer: KLH USA
CLT Installation Specialist: Terry Ducatt
Structural Engineers: AKT II; Bensonwood; PEC Structural; Fire Tower
Civil Engineer: Crescent View Engineering
Associate Architect: Olinger Architects
Façade Research: Alex Timmer
Wood Products Specialist: 7 Seas Group USA
General Contractor: Ryan Locke, Principle Builder's Group
Landscape Design: Carley Rickles
Mechanical Systems: Emily McGlohn
Interior Finishes: Coverings Etc. (Eco-Terr tile); Stone Source (Ornamenta Artwork tile); RPS Distributors (Vives Ceramica Strand-R tile); Rabern-Nash (Johnsonite & Forbo tile)
Wall Assembly: Vapro-Sheild, Vapro-Mat, Kingspan Kooltherm K-20 insulation board
Subcontractors: Cool Roofing Company; Natural Plastering Inc.; RayPaul Coating, Inc.
Photography: Tim Hursley; NAARO

MAURER RESIDENCE
Lead Architects: Florian Maurer, Austin Hawkins
Design Team: Eric Lajoie, Micheal Wetherill, Caspar Viereckel
Clients: Frank + Liz Malinka
Contractor: f2a architecture
Engineering: Fast + Epp Structural Engineers
Collaborators: Geoff Orr, Orr Custom Glazing
Photography: Katie Huisman, Austin Hawkins, Florian Maurer

BRIDGE HOUSE
Architecture Firm: Etienne Design
Design Team: Etienne de Villers
Builder: Luc Trépanier
Photographer: Carl Tessmann

SPRUCE APARTMENTS
Architect: Groupwork (Amin Taha, Dale Elliot, Sam Douek, Nerissa Yeung)
Client: Cobstar Developments
Structural Engineer: Webb Yates
M&E Consultant: Syntegra
Fire Engineering: Optimise
Acoustic Engineering: Syntegra
Project Manager: Groupwork
CDM Coordinator: Syntegra
Building Inspector: MLM

HAUS H
Lead Architects: Pedit & Partner Architekten (Veit Pedit)
Design Team: Veit Pedit, Bettina Lalics, Georg Gruber (ÖBA), Philipp Stiassny
Contractor: ghp gmeiner haferl&partner (Manfred Gmeiner, Martin Haferl)
Photography: Christoph Panzer

CLT HOUSE: FMD
Manufacturers: Fisher & Paykel, In Good Company, Liebherr, Qasir, Smeg, Stora Enso, Tait Flooring, Unlimited Roofing, Wolf, Xlam
Builder: CCB Envico Pty Ltd
Consultants: XLam Australia, Stora Enso
Design Team: Fiona Dunin, Jayme Collins, Bianca Pearson, Rob Kolak, Alex Peck, Andrew Carija, Owen Castley
Structural Engineering: Vistek Engineers

CLT HOUSE: JONES
Architect: atelierjones
Contractor: Cascade Built, Nicole Pi, Terry Ducatt, Al Fernandez, Mark Hughes, Sloan Ritchie, Kirk Hochstatter
Subcontractors: Charles Stratton Cabinets, Sky Hatch, Rubelcon, Siding, Small Planet Workshop, PH Envelope materials, Truescapes, Leader/Fairweather, West Coast Wire and OSP Sling, Katwall Inc., Solar Innovations
Structural Engineering: Harriott, Valentine Engineers, Jim Harriott, Elizabeth Lozner, Jouni Paavola
Photography: Lara Swimmer Photography

HOUTEN HERENHUIS
Architect: Maatworks
Project Architect: Lidewij Lenders
Contractor: Kerkhofs Houtbouw, Henrik-Ido-Ambacht
Structural Engineer: Raadschelders-Bouwadvies
Interior Designer: Maatworks
Kitchen Units and Sanitary Ware: Studio Kwest

GUDBRANDSLIE CABIN
Architecture: Helen & Hard
Manufacturers: Novatop
Photography: Rasmus Norlander, Ragnar Hartvig

THE RYE
Client, Architect, and Main Contractor: Tikari Works
Project Team: Ty Tikari, Nicola Tikari, Nick O'Reilly, Ewelina Krol
Specialist Craftsmen: VT Construct
CLT Subcontractor: Eurban
CLT Manufacturer: Stora Enso
Structural Engineer: Webb Yates
Mechanical and Electrical Engineer: Syntegra
Acoustic Engineer: Syntegra
Approved Building Inspector: MLM
CDM Coordinator: MLM
Planning Consultant: Barton Willmore

R11 LOFT EXTENSION
Architecture Firm: Pool Leber Architekten
Design Team: Isabella Leber, Martin Pool, Johannes Sailer, Valeria Polakovicova
Manufacturers: VELUX Group, LENO, Nemetschek, Rößler & Kannler, Uginox
Photography: Brigida González

BROOKLYN MASS TIMBER HOUSE
Architecture Firm: Schiller Projects
Associate Architect for Landmarks Submission / Stamping: Acheson Doyle Partners
Timber Fabricator: Bensonwood
Windows: Mattison Millworks
Flooring: Tri-Lox
Lighting: Stickbulb
Interior and Exterior Landscape Design: Brook Landscape

AUTHOR'S NOTE

My sincere thanks to Cheryl Weber, who commissioned this book and offered early guidance, as well as to Jesse Marth, my managing editor at Schiffer, who shepherded *Against the Grain* through production to the end. I learned a lot about mass timber as a material strategy, a products industry, and a delivery method from lots of people, notably Amy Stone, Simon Hyoun, Katie Gerfen, Andrew Waugh, Susan Jones, Jennifer Bonner, Nick Milestone, Laure Mériaud, Cécilia Gross, Kyle Hanson, Eran Chen, Chandra Robinson, Andrew Katz, Erich Roden, Joe Allbright, Katie Fernholz, Lauren Wingo, Tom Flicker, Christine Zinkgraf, Rodia Valladares, and others—and I wish to thank each of them for their time and expertise. I've also had opportunities over the last three years to cover mass timber events and projects for *Architect Magazine* and the *Architect's Newspaper*, and I'd like to extend my gratitude to my editors at those publications, including Madeleine D'Angelo, Jack Murphy, and Emily Conklin. Last, but importantly, it was a joy to write about these homes, and I wish to thank all the architects and clients I interviewed whose projects appear in these pages, including the aforementioned Jennifer Bonner, Susan Jones, and Andrew Waugh, as well as Florian Maurer, Austin Hawkins, Etienne de Villers, Jessica Booth, Ben Cox, Veit Pedit, Fiona Dunin, Lidewij Lenders, Reinhard Kropf, Ty Tikari, Isabella Leber, and Aaron Schiller.

For Pascale

WILLIAM RICHARDS is a writer and architectural historian who has covered architecture, communities, design, economics, and urbanism for magazines, journals, and newspapers, including *Architectural Record*, *ARCHITECT Magazine*, *Competitions* magazine, *FRAME*, *Future Anterior*, *Landscape Architecture Magazine*, *Old House Journal*, and others. He is the author of four books about architecture, including *Together by Design: The Art & Architecture of Communal Living* (Princeton Architectural Press, 2022), *Bamboo Contemporary: Green Houses around the Globe* (Princeton Architectural Press, 2022), and *Revolt and Reform in Architecture's Academy: Urban Renewal, Race, and the Rise of Design in the Public Interest* (Routledge/Taylor & Francis, 2017). He holds a PhD in the history of art and architecture from the University of Virginia.